Step Back in Time

Turn Reproduction Prints into Vintage-Inspired Quilts

Paula Barnes and Mary Ellen Robison
of Red Crinoline Quilts

D1614116

Martingale®
Create with Confidence

Step Back in Time:
Turn Reproduction Prints into Vintage-Inspired Quilts
© 2019 by Paula Barnes and Mary Ellen Robison

Martingale®
19021 120th Ave. NE, Ste. 102
Bothell, WA 98011-9511 USA
ShopMartingale.com

Printed in China
24 23 22 21 20 19   8 7 6 5 4 3 2 1

Library of Congress Cataloging-in-Publication Data
Names: Barnes, Paula, author. | Robison, Mary Ellen, author.
Title: Step back in time : turn reproduction prints into vintage-inspired quilts / Paula Barnes and Mary Ellen Robison.
Description: Bothell, WA : Martingale, [2019]
Identifiers: LCCN 2018032709 | ISBN 9781604689051
Subjects: LCSH: Patchwork quilts. | Patchwork--Patterns. | United States--History--19th century--Anecdotes.
Classification: LCC T1835 .B27165 2019 | DDC 746.46/041--dc23
LC record available at https://lccn.loc.gov/2018032709

MISSION STATEMENT

We empower makers who use fabric and yarn
to make life more enjoyable.

CREDITS

PUBLISHER AND
CHIEF VISIONARY OFFICER
Jennifer Erbe Keltner

CONTENT DIRECTOR
Karen Costello Soltys

DESIGN MANAGER
Adrienne Smitke

MANAGING EDITOR
Tina Cook

PRODUCTION MANAGER
Regina Girard

ACQUISITIONS EDITOR
Amelia Johanson

INTERIOR DESIGNER
Angie Hoogensen

TECHNICAL EDITOR
Ellen Pahl

PHOTOGRAPHERS
Brent Kane
Adam Albright

COPY EDITOR
Sheila Chapman Ryan

ILLUSTRATOR
Sandy Loi

PHOTOGRAPH CREDITS
The vintage photographs in this book are in
the public domain or used by permission.

SPECIAL THANKS
*Photography for this book was taken at
Tracy Fish's Fishtail Cottage in Kenmore, Washington,
and at the home of Julie Smiley of Des Moines, Iowa.*

DEDICATION

*To our families! Thank you for your love
and support throughout our journey.*

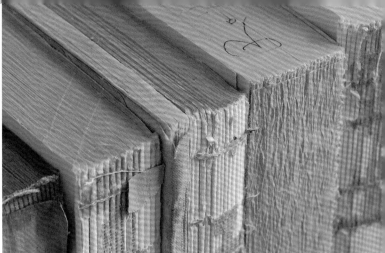

CONTENTS

INTRODUCTION

Many of you, our loyal friends, already know our story. We're friends, quilt lovers, and fabric hoarders, and a desire to share all of this with our fellow quilters led us to open Red Crinoline Quilts, an online store specializing in reproduction fabric and quilt patterns. It began around a kitchen table in Katy, Texas, in 2005, and now after 14 years in business together, our passion for quilting has remained and our friendship has grown.

Step Back in Time showcases our love for scrappy quilts that feature reproduction fabrics, as well as our love for both large and small projects. Though we're known for our big quilts, we're always excited to find the time to complete a smaller, easier project. If we just described you, then this book will meet your needs. After all, who doesn't like crossing a project off the list?

While all of the quilts featured in this book are pieced with reproduction fabrics, there's no reason why other fabrics can't be used. Try some of the quilts with batiks or bright fabrics, but we recommend keeping the overall theme scrappy. We love the look of a scrappy quilt, whether it's totally scrappy, as in A House Divided (page 72), The Quilting Bee (page 38), and Kentucky Baskets (page 64), or it's "controlled scrappy" (only a couple colors are used), as in Smithson's Legacy (page 78), The Harvey Girls (page 24), and Pioneer Life (page 84).

Many of the large quilts will take some time to piece, but just think of the scraps they'll use up! All of the quilts are easily made from smaller pieces of fabric—scraps, strips, or fat quarters. It's time to break apart your fat-quarter bundles, dig into your scrap bins, and create an heirloom quilt of your own.

We hope you enjoy your new quilt designs, surely soon to become family treasures.

BLUE RIDGE MOUNTAINS

At over one billion years old, the Blue Ridge Mountains are one of the oldest mountain ranges in the world. Part of the Appalachians, the Blue Ridge is divided by the Roanoke River gap into the northern and southern sections and crosses eight states: Pennsylvania, Maryland, Virginia, West Virginia, Tennessee, North Carolina, South Carolina, and Georgia. It is home to two major parks— the Shenandoah National Park in the northern section, and the Great Smoky Mountains National Park in the southern section—as well as the Blue Ridge Parkway, a 469-mile-long scenic highway that connects the two parks. The highest peak east of the Rockies is in the Blue Ridge Mountains; Mount Mitchell in North Carolina is 6,684 feet high.

The "blue" that the mountains are famous for, and that can be seen from a distance, is from the hydrocarbons the mountain forests release into the atmosphere. A temperate climate and the gentle, rolling mountains caused by years of erosion made these mountains very accessible and appealing to the first settlers. As Thomas Jefferson said when he first saw the Blue Ridge, "It is impossible for the emotions arising from the sublime to be felt beyond what they are here … The rapture of the spectator is really indescribable."

The Blue Ridge Mountains were home to numerous Native American people in both Virginia and what is now the Great Smoky Mountains National Park. They were also the site for several Civil War skirmishes. Today, the Appalachian Trail, which follows the Blue Ridge Mountains in Virginia, is a favorite destination for hikers.

The Blue Ridge Mountains.
KEN THOMAS, WIKIMEDIA COMMONS

BLUE RIDGE MOUNTAINS

FINISHED QUILT 50½" × 50½" ◆ **FINISHED BLOCK** 6" × 6"

Designed and pieced by Paula Barnes; quilted by Sharon Dixon

Materials

Yardage is based on 42"-wide fabric.

- ¼ yard *each* of 9 assorted light prints for blocks*
- ¼ yard *each* of 9 assorted dark prints for blocks*
- ¼ yard of tan print for inner border
- 1⅝ yards of striped print for outer border
- ½ yard of fabric for binding
- 3¼ yards of fabric for backing
- 57" × 57" piece of batting
- 1½" finished Star Singles papers (optional)**

You can also use fat quarters.

**See "Using Star Singles" below right before cutting fabrics.*

Cutting

From *each* of the 9 light prints, cut:
2 squares, 5¾" × 5¾" (18 total)
12 squares, 2¾" × 2¾" (108 total)
4 squares, 2" × 2" (36 total)

From *each* of the 9 dark prints, cut:
2 squares, 5¾" × 5¾" (18 total)
12 squares, 2¾" × 2¾" (108 total)

From the tan print, cut:
4 strips, 1½" × 42"; crosscut into:
    2 strips, 1½" × 36½"
    2 strips, 1½" × 38½"

From the striped print, cut on the *lengthwise* grain:
4 strips, 6½" × 55½"

From the binding fabric, cut:
6 strips, 1⅞" × 42"

USING STAR SINGLES

If you use the 1½" Star Singles papers, do not cut the 2¾" squares from the light and dark prints. Instead, skip step 1 of "Making the Blocks" on page 10 and follow the directions on the package to cut the following pieces.

From *each* of the 9 assorted light prints, cut:
3 squares, 5½" × 5½" (27 total)

From *each* of the 9 assorted dark prints, cut:
3 squares, 5½" × 5½" (27 total)

Making the Blocks

Press the seam allowances as indicated by the arrows in the illustrations.

1 Referring to "Half-Square-Triangle Units" on page 92, mark the light 2¾" squares and layer them right sides together with the dark 2¾" squares. Sew, cut, press, and trim to 2" square. Make 216 half-square-triangle units.

Make 216 units.

2 Repeat step 1 with the assorted light and dark 5¾" squares to make 36 half-square-triangle units. Trim the units to measure 5" square.

 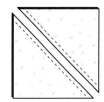

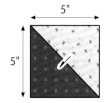

Make 36 units.

3 Sew three half-square-triangle units from step 1 together as shown. Make 36 units. Repeat to make 36 units with the triangles going in the opposite direction. The units should measure 2" × 5", including seam allowances.

Make 36 of each unit,
2" × 5".

4 Arrange one of each unit from step 3 together with a half-square-triangle unit from step 2 and a light 2" square as shown. Sew the units into rows and then sew the rows together to complete the block. Make 36 blocks that measure 6½" square, including seam allowances.

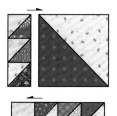 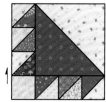

Make 36 blocks,
6½" × 6½".

Constructing the Quilt

1 Arrange the blocks into six rows of six blocks each, alternating the position of each block as shown. Sew the blocks into rows and then sew the rows together. The quilt center should measure 36½" square, including seam allowances.

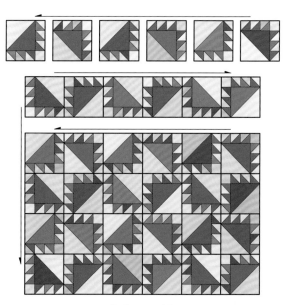

Quilt assembly

2 Sew the tan 1½" × 36½" strips to the sides of the quilt. Sew the 1½" × 38½" strips to the top and bottom. The quilt center should measure 38½" square, including seam allowances.

3 Referring to "Mitered Borders" on page 93, add the striped 6½" × 55½" strips to all four sides of the quilt and miter the corners. The quilt top should measure 50½" square.

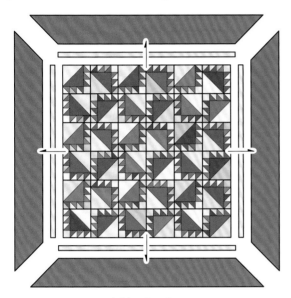

Adding borders

Finishing the Quilt

For help with any of the finishing steps, go to ShopMartingale.com/HowtoQuilt.

1 Layer the quilt top with the batting and backing. Quilt by hand or machine. The quilt shown is machine quilted in an overall feather design.

2 Make the binding using the 1⅞"-wide strips and attach it to the quilt.

WILD ROSE

Rose O'Neal Greenhow was the Confederacy's most famous female spy. She was born Maria Rosatta O'Neale to a large slave-holding family in Virginia in 1814. As a young girl, Rose and her sisters moved to Washington, DC, to live with an aunt who ran a boardinghouse. Rose had an active social life, rubbing shoulders with influential men like her future husband, wealthy Virginian Dr. Robert Greenhow.

The Greenhows moved to San Francisco, but Dr. Greenhow died shortly after their arrival. Rose and the children moved back to Washington, DC, where she established herself in the city's social circles as a powerful person, someone able to influence people in political power.

In 1860, as tensions increased, Rose became a staunch supporter and activist for the Confederacy. As a popular and powerful Washington hostess, Rose moved with grace and ease among the Washington elite. When the war began in 1861, she used this influence and charm to gain intelligence information from the Union that she then passed on to Confederate leaders. Rumor has it that information she obtained about Union troop movements helped the Confederate troops in the first battle of Bull Run. Confederate President Jefferson Davis thanked her for her help and support.

Rose continued to spy for the Confederacy, but her actions drew the attention of Federal officials. In August 1861, she and her youngest daughter, Little Rose, were placed under house arrest. But even with her house surrounded by Union guards, she was still able to pass along information. She and Little Rose were sent to Old Capital Prison and finally banished farther south. They eventually moved to England, where Rose still worked in support of the Confederacy and even wrote a book about her imprisonment.

She traveled back to America in 1864 aboard the blockade-runner *Condor*, but the ship ran aground off the coast of North Carolina. Despite poor weather conditions, Rose insisted upon boarding a rowboat to complete the trip. Unfortunately, the ship sank, and Rose drowned—weighed down by gold coins, the royalties from her book, which she refused to leave behind.

"Wild Rose" was honored with a Confederate military funeral and was buried in Wilmington, North Carolina, on October 1, 1864. Her headstone reads, "Mrs. Rose O'N. Greenhow, a bearer of dispatches to the Confederate government."

Rose O'Neal Greenhow with daughter, 1862.
WIKIMEDIA COMMONS

WILD ROSE

FINISHED QUILT 47⅝" × 47⅝" ◆ **FINISHED BLOCK** 4½" × 4½"
Designed by Paula Barnes; pieced by Mary Ellen Robison;
quilted by Cathy Peters of Palm Tree Quilting

Materials

Yardage is based on 42"-wide fabric; fat quarters measure 18" × 21".

- 15 scraps, at least 6" × 21", of assorted light prints for blocks
- 15 scraps, at least 6" × 21", of assorted dark prints for blocks
- ⅜ yard of pink print for alternate blocks
- 1 fat quarter of tan print for alternate blocks
- 1 yard of dark floral for borders*
- ½ yard of fabric for binding
- 3 yards of fabric for backing
- 54" × 54" piece of batting
- 1½" finished Star Singles papers (optional)**

If you want to use the same dark floral for binding, you'll need 1⅜ yards.

**See "Using Star Singles" below right before cutting fabrics.*

Cutting

From *each* of the 15 assorted light prints, cut:
12 squares, 2¾" × 2¾" (180 total)

From *each* of the 15 assorted dark prints, cut:
12 squares, 2¾" × 2¾" (180 total)

From the pink print, cut:
2 strips, 5" × 42"; crosscut into 15 squares, 5" × 5"

From the tan print, cut:
10 squares, 5" × 5"

From the dark floral, cut:
4 strips, 5" × 42"
5 squares, 7⅝" × 7⅝"; cut in quarters diagonally to make 20 triangles
2 squares, 4⅛" × 4⅛"; cut in half diagonally to make 4 triangles

From the binding fabric, cut:
5 strips, 1⅞" × 42"

USING STAR SINGLES

If you want to use 1½" finished Star Singles papers, do not cut the 2¾" squares. Instead, skip step 1 of "Making the Blocks" on page 16 and follow the directions on the package to cut the following pieces.

From *each* of the 15 light prints, cut:
3 squares, 5½" × 5½" (45 total)

From *each* of the 15 dark prints, cut:
3 squares, 5½" × 5½" (45 total)

Making the Blocks

Press the seam allowances as indicated by the arrows in the illustrations.

1. Referring to "Half-Square-Triangle Units" on page 92, mark the light 2¾" squares and layer them right sides together with the dark squares. Sew, cut, press, and trim to 2" × 2". Make a total of 360 half-square-triangle units.

Make 360 units.

2. Arrange and sew nine half-square-triangle units together to make three rows. Sew the rows together to create a block. Repeat to make a total of 40 blocks that measure 5" square, including seam allowances. Make the blocks as scrappy as possible.

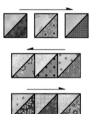

Make 40 blocks, 5" × 5".

CHECK YOUR SEAM ALLOWANCE

Before beginning any quilt, please make sure you're sewing a correct ¼" seam allowance. To check this, refer to "Skills" on page 91 and follow the steps to sew three 1½" × 4" strips together. It's worth the extra time to find the correct seam allowance on your machine.

Constructing the Quilt

1. Arrange the pieced blocks and the pink and tan alternate blocks together in diagonal rows as shown in the quilt assembly diagram below. Set aside four blocks to use in the border corners.

2. Sew the blocks and alternate blocks together in rows. Add the floral side triangles to the end of each row as indicated. Sew the rows together and add the floral corner triangles last. The quilt center should measure approximately 38⅝" square, including seam allowances.

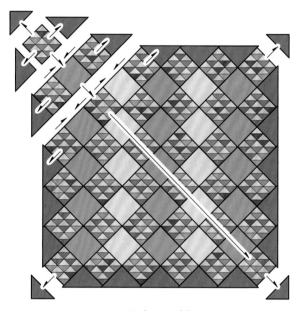

Quilt assembly

3 Measure the quilt center and cut the four dark floral 5" × 42" strips to that measurement. Sew border strips to opposite sides of the quilt top. Sew a block set aside in step 1 to each end of the remaining two border strips, noting the orientation of the block. Sew them to the top and bottom of the quilt. The quilt top should measure approximately 47⅝" square.

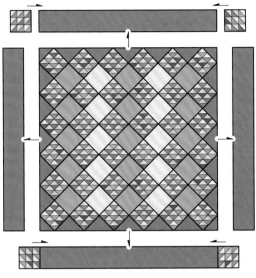

Adding borders

Finishing the Quilt

For help with any of the finishing steps, go to ShopMartingale.com/HowtoQuilt.

1 Layer the quilt top with the batting and backing. Quilt by hand or machine. The quilt shown is quilted in an overall meandering design.

2 Make the binding using the 1⅞"-wide strips and attach it to the quilt.

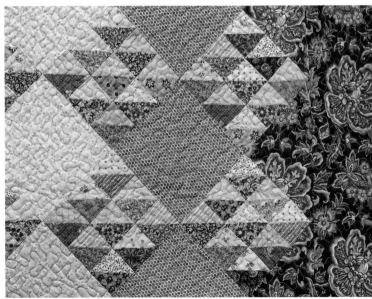

WOODEN SHIPS

No matter the type of wooden ship or "tall ship," they all have the same basic characteristics: a hull, rigging, at least one mast, and sails that use wind to power the ship. Wind power meant the ships lacked speed, and journeys on these ships would take many months and face many hazards, including lack of wind, powerful storms, shipwrecks, pirates, and disease. Wind power also meant these ships were limited in size—a maximum of 14,000 tons displacement. Space for cargo and passengers was small, and this caused additional problems with providing enough provisions for both the crew and passengers. Food and fresh water were often in short supply.

Frigates and sloops were just two of the wooden ships that were active in wartime during the 1800s. The *USS Constitution*, or "Old Ironsides," is the oldest commissioned warship that is still afloat and can be seen in Charleston, Massachusetts. It survived British cannonballs bouncing off its oak hull during the War of 1812.

At the Battle of Hampton Roads in March 1862, the *CSS Virginia*, a Confederate Ironclad warship, faced a squadron of five Union wooden warships, among them the *USS Cumberland*. The Union warships fired on the *Virginia*, but their cannonballs had no effect on the ironclad *Virginia*. The *Virginia* fired back at the wooden ships, but most of the damage the *Cumberland* suffered was when the *Virginia* rammed it with its iron ram. The sinking of the *USS Cumberland* signaled the end of the wooden sailing warship. Some of these ships have been restored to their original beauty and can be seen at maritime museums. Modern-day tall ships can be seen in tall ship races around the world.

USS Constitution, attributed to Michele Felice Corné, 1803.
WIKIMEDIA COMMONS

WOODEN SHIPS

FINISHED QUILT 29½" × 29½" ◆ **FINISHED BLOCK** 7" × 7"
Designed and pieced by Paula Barnes;
quilted by Marcella Pickett of Crooked Creek Quilts

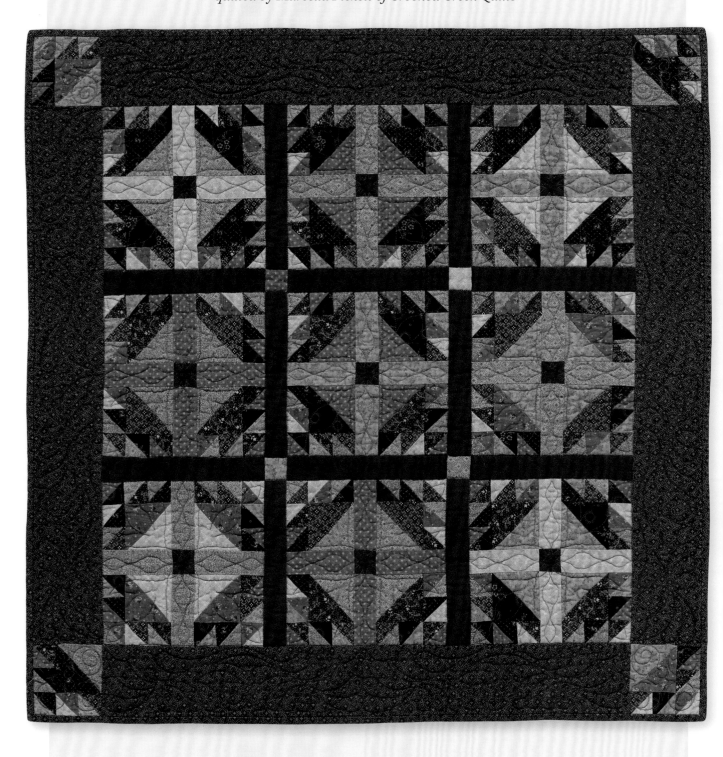

Materials

Yardage is based on 42"-wide fabric; fat quarters measure 18" × 21".

- 5 fat quarters of assorted light prints for blocks and sashing squares*
- 5 fat quarters of assorted dark prints for blocks*
- ¼ yard of dark brown print for sashing and block centers
- ½ yard of blue print for border**
- ⅜ yard of fabric for binding
- 1 yard of fabric for backing
- 34" × 34" piece of batting
- 1" and 2" finished Star Singles papers (optional)***

You can also use 5 assorted ¼-yard cuts.

**If you want to use the same blue print for binding, you'll need ¾ yard.*

***See "Using Star Singles" below right before cutting fabrics.*

Cutting

From *each* of the 5 assorted light prints, cut:
4 squares, 3¼" × 3¼" (20 total)
20 squares, 2¼" × 2¼" (100 total)
8 rectangles, 1½" × 3½" (40 total; 4 are extra)
1 square, 1½" × 1½" (5 total; 1 is extra)

From *each* of the 5 assorted dark prints, cut:
4 squares, 3¼" × 3¼" (20 total)
20 squares, 2¼" × 2¼" (100 total)

From the dark brown print, cut:
3 strips, 1½" × 42"; crosscut into:
    12 rectangles, 1½" × 7½"
    9 squares, 1½" × 1½"

From the blue print, cut:
4 strips, 3½" × 23½"

From the binding fabric, cut:
4 strips, 1⅞" × 42"

USING STAR SINGLES

If you want to use 1" and 2" finished Star Singles papers, do not cut the 2¼" and 3¼" squares from the assorted lights and darks. Instead, skip step 1 of "Making the Blocks" on page 22 and follow the directions on the package to cut the following pieces.

From *each* light print, cut:
1 square, 6½" × 6½" (5 total)
5 squares, 4½" × 4½" (25 total)

From *each* dark print, cut:
1 square, 6½" × 6½" (5 total)
5 squares, 4½" × 4½" (25 total)

2 Repeat step 1 to mark the light 2¼" squares and layer them right sides together with the dark 2¼" squares. Sew, cut, press, and then trim to 1½" square. Make a total of 200 half-square-triangle units.

Make 200 units.

3 Arrange and sew five units from step 2 and one unit from step 1 together in rows as shown. Sew the rows together to create a block unit that measures 3½" square, including seam allowances. Make a total of 40 block units, mixing and matching fabrics to make them as scrappy as possible. Set four of the block units aside to use in the border corners.

Make 40 units,
3½" × 3½".

4 Arrange and sew four block units that have matching large light triangles, four matching light 1½" × 3½" rectangles, and one dark brown 1½" square together in rows as shown. Sew the rows together to make a block that measures 7½" square, including seam allowances. Make a total of nine blocks.

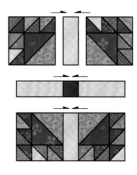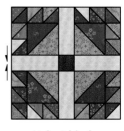

Make 9 blocks,
7½" × 7½".

Making the Blocks

Press the seam allowances as indicated by the arrows in the illustrations.

1 Referring to "Half-Square-Triangle Units" on page 92, mark the light 3¼" squares and layer them right sides together with the dark 3¼" squares. Sew, cut, press, and then trim to 2½" square. Make a total of 40 half-square-triangle units.

Make 40 units.

Constructing the Quilt

1 Arrange the blocks, the dark brown 1½" × 7½" sashing rectangles, and the light 1½" sashing squares into rows as shown. Sew the blocks and sashing into rows and then sew the sashing rectangles and sashing squares together to create two sashing rows. Join the rows to make the quilt center, which should measure 23½" square, including seam allowances.

2 Sew blue 3½" × 23½" strips to opposite sides of the quilt top. Sew a block unit to each end of the remaining blue print border strips, noting the orientation of the half-square-triangle units. Sew the borders to the top and bottom of the quilt top, which should measure 29½" square.

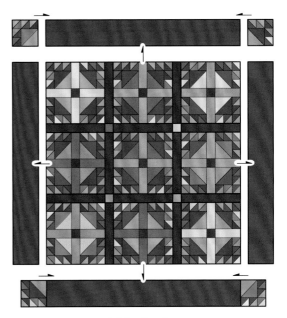

Adding borders

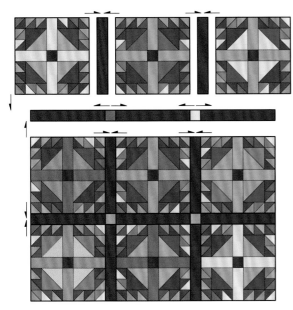

Quilt assembly

Finishing the Quilt

For help with any of the finishing steps, go to ShopMartingale.com/HowtoQuilt.

1 Layer the quilt top with the batting and backing. Quilt by hand or machine. The quilt shown is machine quilted with a floral design in the blocks and a feathered vine in the border.

2 Make the binding using the 1⅞"-wide strips and attach it to the quilt.

THE VINTAGE LOOK

To achieve the look of an antique quilt, stitch your blocks in reproduction fabrics. Layer the finished quilt top with a low-loft cotton or cotton-blend batting and quilt. After adding the binding, machine wash the quilt in hot or warm water. Place it in the dryer, and when you remove the quilt, it will be soft and puckered—just like a coveted antique.

THE HARVEY GIRLS

The phrase "Go West, young man" is often credited to Horace Greeley, an American author and newspaper editor. But the phrase was most likely first stated by John Babson Lane Soule and later used by Greeley in an editorial in 1865. Greeley was a strong supporter and leading voice in America's westward expansion.

Unfortunately, the trip West was full of peril. The railroad was one of the safest ways to travel, but it was very unpleasant. A trip from New York to California could easily take a week in hot, uncomfortable train cars with food, if available, that tasted horrible and was often spoiled.

Railroad agent Fred Harvey saw an opportunity, and in 1876 he began a partnership with the ATSF (Atchison, Topeka and Santa Fe), America's largest railroad company, to provide restaurants and eventually hotels along their Western routes. With low populations in most of the towns, Harvey's first problem was locating staff to work in his Harvey Houses.

Harvey ran ads in Midwest and East Coast newspapers for "Young women, 18–30 years of age, of good character,

attractive and intelligent." Wages were $17.50 a month, and room and board were provided. Applicants were interviewed by Mrs. Harvey and when hired, placed in a six-week training program.

Harvey was a stickler for rules, and he demanded that his restaurants provide exemplary food and service for all his customers. Members of the all-female waitstaff were called "Harvey Girls." They dressed in the same impeccable black-and-white uniforms, lived in dormitories, followed curfews, and agreed to remain single for the duration of their six-month contract. It is estimated that of the over 100,000 girls hired, 20,000 became wives of their customers. Will Rogers said, "They kept the West in food and wives."

With the decline in railroad travel and the inventions of the automobile and airplane, Harvey Houses began to close. They had provided a great service to both the men and women of the West.

A "Harvey Girl" uniform on display at the Arizona Railroad Museum.
JOT POWERS, WIKIMEDIA COMMONS

THE HARVEY GIRLS

FINISHED QUILT 36½" × 36½" ◆ **FINISHED BLOCK** 6" × 6"

Designed and pieced by Paula Barnes;
quilted by Marcella Pickett of Crooked Creek Quilts

Materials

Yardage is based on 42"-wide fabric; fat quarters measure 18" × 21".

- 4 fat quarters of assorted navy prints and black prints for blocks (collectively referred to as *navy*)*
- ⅔ yard of tan print for blocks
- ⅓ yard of red print for blocks and sashing
- ⅜ yard of brown print for sashing and inner border
- ⅝ yard of black print for outer border
- ⅜ yard of fabric for binding
- 2½ yards of fabric for backing
- 43" × 43" piece of batting
- 1½" finished Star Singles papers (optional)**

*You can also use ¼-yard cuts.

**See "Using Star Singles" at right before cutting fabrics.

Cutting

From *each* of the 4 assorted navy prints, cut:
16 squares, 2¾" × 2¾" (64 total)
16 squares, 2" × 2" (64 total)

From the tan print, cut:
5 strips, 2¾" × 42"; crosscut into 64 squares, 2¾" × 2¾"
4 strips, 1½" × 42"; crosscut into:
    8 rectangles, 1½" × 13"
    4 rectangles, 1½" × 8"

From the red print, cut:
5 strips, 1½" × 42"; crosscut into:
    4 rectangles, 1½" × 13"
    8 rectangles, 1½" × 8"
    4 squares, 1½" × 1½"
    4 rectangles, 1½" × 13½"

From the brown print, cut:
7 strips, 1½" × 42"; crosscut into:
    16 rectangles, 1½" × 6½"
    2 strips, 1½" × 27½"
    2 strips, 1½" × 29½"
    1 square, 1½" × 1½"

From the black print, cut:
2 strips, 4" × 29½"
2 strips, 4" × 36½"

From the binding fabric, cut:
4 strips, 1⅞" × 42"

USING STAR SINGLES

If you want to use 1½" finished Star Singles papers, do not cut the 2¾" squares from the navy prints and the tan print. Instead, skip step 1 of "Making the Blocks" below and follow the directions on the package to cut the following pieces.

From *each* of the 4 assorted navy prints, cut:
4 squares, 5½" × 5½" (16 total)

From the tan print, cut:
16 squares, 5½" × 5½"

Making the Blocks

Press the seam allowances as indicated by the arrows in the illustrations.

1 Referring to "Half-Square-Triangle Units" on page 92, mark the tan 2¾" squares and layer them right sides together with the navy 2¾" squares. Sew, cut, press, and then trim to 2" square. Make a total of 128 half-square-triangle units.

Make 128 units.

2 Sew two different half-square-triangle units together to create a star-point unit. Make a total of 64 star-point units.

Make 64 units,
2" × 3½".

3 Sew two tan 1½" × 13" strips and one red 1½" × 13" strip together. Make four strip sets. Cut into 32 segments that measure 1½" wide.

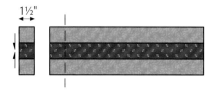

Make 4 strip sets, 3½" × 13".
Cut 32 segments, 1½" × 3½".

SHORT AND SWEET

Cutting and sewing shorter strips when working with strip sets makes them easier to sew and press. The shorter lengths allow you to maintain control when pressing to keep the strip sets uniform and straight.

---

4 Sew a tan 1½" × 8" strip and two red 1½" × 8" strips together. Make four strip sets. Cut into 16 total segments that measure 1½" wide.

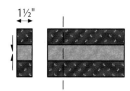

Make 4 strip sets, 3½" × 8".
Cut 16 segments, 1½" × 3½".

5 Sew two segments from step 3 together with a segment from step 4 to create a nine-patch unit that measures 3½" square, including seam allowances. Make 16 units.

Make 16 units,
3½" × 3½".

6 Arrange and sew four navy 2" squares, four star-point units, and one nine-patch unit together into three rows as shown. Sew the rows together to make a block that measures 6½" square, including seam allowances. Make a total of 16 Star blocks.

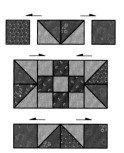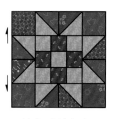

Make 16 blocks,
6½" × 6½".

Constructing the Quilt

1 Sew four Star blocks, one red 1½" square, and four brown 1½" × 6½" rectangles together into rows. Sew the rows together to make a four-block section that measures 13½" square, including seam allowances. Make four four-block sections.

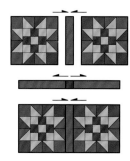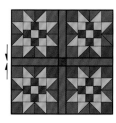

Make 4 sections,
13½" × 13½".

2 Arrange and sew the four red 1½" × 13½" sashing rectangles, the four-block sections, and the brown 1½" square to create three rows. Sew the rows together to create the quilt center that measures 27½" square, including seam allowances.

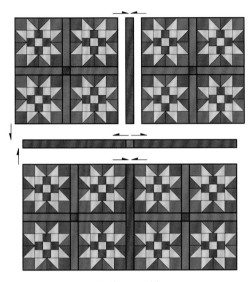

Quilt assembly

3 Sew the brown 1½" × 27½" strips to the sides of the quilt. Sew the brown 1½" × 29½" strips to the top and bottom.

4 Sew the black 4" × 29½" strips to the sides of the quilt. Sew the black 4" × 36½" strips to the top and bottom. The quilt top should measure 36½" square.

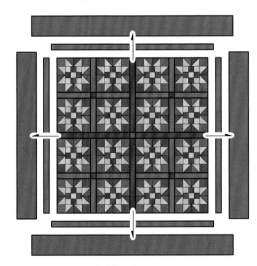

Adding borders

Finishing the Quilt

For help with any of the finishing steps, go to ShopMartingale.com/HowtoQuilt.

1 Layer the quilt top with the batting and backing. Quilt by hand or machine. The quilt shown is machine quilted with a feathered wreath design in the blocks and a feathered vine in the border.

2 Make the binding using the 1⅞"-wide strips and attach it to the quilt.

HEROINES OF THE PAST

On Election Day in 1920, millions of American women voted for the first time because of the efforts of men and women over the previous 100 years. These were men and women who made speeches, marched in parades, signed petitions, and were even imprisoned. While they didn't always agree with one another on some issues, they all agreed that women deserved the right to vote. The five most prominent leaders in the women's suffrage movement were Susan B. Anthony (1820–1906), Alice Paul (1885–1977), Elizabeth Cady Stanton (1815–1902), Lucy Stone (1818–1893), and Ida B. Wells (1862–1931). Alice Paul and Ida B. Wells were the only two to see the Nineteenth Amendment adopted on August 18, 1920, and to be among the first women to vote.

In addition to being founders and supporters of the women's suffrage movement, these women were well-known activists in the history of women's rights. Susan B. Anthony was a temperance activist, an abolitionist, and a supporter of the expansion of married women's rights to property. Alice Paul was the leader of the most militant wing of the movement and was imprisoned for staging a seven-month picket outside the White House. Elizabeth Cady Stanton was also an abolitionist. In 1848, she and Lucretia Mott organized the first women's rights convention in Seneca Falls, New York, marking the beginning of the movement. Lucy Stone, also an abolitionist, is most known for refusing to change her last name when she married fellow activist Henry Blackwell in 1855. Ida B. Wells is best known for being a journalist for the Memphis black newspaper, *The Free Speech*, and an anti-lynching activist.

It was on the shoulders and backs of these women and many others that women received the right to vote in 1920.

The Portrait Monument, featuring Elizabeth Cady Stanton, Susan B. Anthony, and Lucretia Mott.
WIKIMEDIA COMMONS

HEROINES OF THE PAST

FINISHED QUILT 83" × 85⅜" ◆ **FINISHED BLOCKS** 6" × 6" and 8" × 8"

Designed by Paula Barnes; pieced by Mary Ellen Robison;
quilted by Marcella Pickett of Crooked Creek Quilts

Materials

Yardage is based on 42"-wide fabric.

- ½ yard *each* of 8 assorted light prints for blocks
- ½ yard *each* of 8 assorted dark prints for blocks
- 6 scraps, 5" × 5" *each*, of assorted medium prints for blocks
- 2⅞ yards of red print for setting triangles
- 2½ yards of cream print for sashing
- ⅔ yard of fabric for binding
- 8 yards of fabric for backing
- 91" × 94" piece of batting
- 2" finished Star Singles papers (optional)*

*See "Using Star Singles" below right before cutting fabrics.

Cutting

From *each* of the 8 assorted light prints, cut:
2 strips, 3¼" × 42"; crosscut into 22 squares,
   3¼" × 3¼" (176 total)
2 squares, 4½" × 4½" (16 total)
4 squares, 2½" × 2½" (32 total)

From *each of* 6 of the assorted light prints, cut:
1 square, 3¾" × 3¾" (6 total)
4 squares, 2½" × 2½" (24 total)

From *each of* 7 of the assorted light prints, cut:
2 rectangles, 2½" × 11" (14 total)
1 rectangle, 2½" × 6" (7 total)

From *each* of the 8 assorted dark prints, cut:
2 strips, 3¼" × 42"; crosscut into 22 squares,
   3¼" × 3¼" (176 total)
8 squares, 2½" × 2½" (64 total)

From *each of* 6 of the assorted dark prints, cut:
2 squares, 3¾" × 3¾" (12 total)
1 square, 2½" × 2½" (6 total)

From *each of* 7 of the assorted dark prints, cut:
1 rectangle, 2½" × 11" (7 total)
2 rectangles, 2½" × 6" (14 total)

From *each* of the 6 assorted medium prints, cut:
1 square, 3¾" × 3¾" (6 total)

From the red print, cut:
14 squares, 12⅝" × 12⅝"; cut into quarters
   diagonally to make 56 large triangles
9 squares, 9¾" × 9¾"; cut into quarters diagonally
   to make 36 small triangles
4 squares, 6⅝" × 6⅝"; cut in half diagonally to
   make 8 large corner triangles
4 squares, 5½" × 5½"; cut in half diagonally to
   make 8 small corner triangles

From the cream print, cut on the *lengthwise* grain:*
4 strips, 3½" × 85⅜" strips
2 strips, 4½" × 85⅜"

From the binding fabric, cut:
9 strips, 1⅞" × 42"

*It's best to wait until the block rows are pieced and measured before cutting the vertical sashing strips.

USING STAR SINGLES

If you want to use 2" finished Star Singles papers, do not cut the 3¼" squares. Instead, skip "Making the Half-Square-Triangle Units" on page 34 and follow the directions on the package to cut the following pieces.

From *each* of the 8 assorted light prints, cut:
5 squares, 6½" × 6½" (40 total)

From *each* of the 8 assorted dark prints, cut:
5 squares, 6½" × 6½" (40 total)

Cut 1 additional square from each of 4 lights and 4 darks so that you have a total of 44 light squares and 44 dark squares.

Making the Half-Square-Triangle Units

Press the seam allowances as indicated by the arrows in the illustrations.

Referring to "Half-Square-Triangle Units" on page 92, mark the light 3¼" squares and layer them right sides together with the dark 3¼" squares. Sew, cut, press, and then trim to 2½" square. Make a total of 352 half-square-triangle units. You'll need 160 units for the Anvil blocks and 192 units for the Sixteen Patch blocks.

Make 352 units.

Making the Anvil Blocks

Sew 10 matching half-square-triangle units, two matching light 2½" squares, and a matching light 4½" square together in three rows. Sew the rows together and press to make an Anvil block that measures 8½" square, including seam allowances. Make 16 blocks.

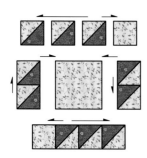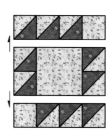

Make 16 blocks,
8½" × 8½".

Making the 16-Patch Blocks

Sew 12 assorted half-square-triangle units and four assorted dark 2½" squares together into four rows. Sew the rows together and press to make a Sixteen Patch block measuring 8½" square, including seam allowances. Make 16 blocks.

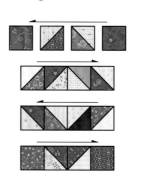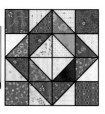

Make 16 blocks,
8½" × 8½".

Making the Star Blocks

1 For one block, choose the following pieces:

- 1 light 3¾" square
- 1 medium 3¾" square
- 2 matching dark 3¾" squares
- 4 matching light 2½" squares
- 1 dark 2½" square

2 With a pencil, draw two diagonal lines from corner to corner on the wrong side of the light 3¾" square and the medium 3¾" square, making an X.

3 Place a marked light and a dark 3¾" square right sides together. Sew ¼" on both sides of *one* of the pencil lines. Cut on both pencil lines and press to make four units.

Make 4 units.

4 Repeat step 3 with a marked medium and a dark 3¾" square to make four units.

Make 4 units.

5 Sew a unit from step 3 to a unit from step 4 to create an hourglass unit. Make four identical hourglass units. Refer to "Trimming Hourglass Units" at right to trim the units to 2½" square.

2½"

2½"

Make 4 units.

6 Arrange and sew four hourglass units, four matching light 2½" squares, and one dark 2½" square together into three rows as shown. Sew the rows together to make a Star block that measures 6½" square, including seam allowances. Repeat the steps to make six blocks.

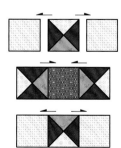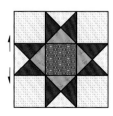

Make 6 blocks, 6½" × 6½".

TRIMMING HOURGLASS UNITS

We like to make hourglass units oversized and trim them after sewing. This guarantees that the units will be the exact size needed.

1 Place a square ruler on top of the block, aligning the 45° line of the ruler with the diagonal seam line of the hourglass unit. Divide the desired trimmed size of the block by two and make sure those lines of the ruler meet at the center of the block. For the 2½" unfinished units, place the 1¼" lines at the center of the unit. The 2½" lines of the ruler should line up with the opposite diagonal seam of the hourglass unit.

2 Trim the unit along the top and right edges of the ruler.

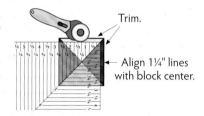

Trim.

Align 1¼" lines with block center.

3 Rotate the unit so that the newly trimmed sides align with the 2½" lines of the ruler and the 45° line of the ruler is aligned with the diagonal seam line of the hourglass unit. The 1¼" lines should meet in the center of the block as in step 1.

4 Trim the unit along the top and right edges of the ruler. You now have a perfect hourglass unit.

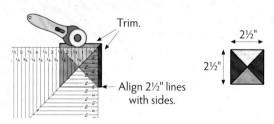

Trim.

Align 2½" lines with sides.

2½"

2½"

Making the Nine Patch Blocks

1 Choose the following pieces from *one* light print and *one* dark print to make two identical blocks at a time:

- ◆ 2 light 2½" × 11" rectangles
- ◆ 1 light 2½" × 6" rectangle
- ◆ 1 dark 2½" × 11" rectangle
- ◆ 2 dark 2½" × 6" rectangles

2 Sew two matching light and one dark 2½" × 11" rectangle together to make a strip set. Cut the strip into four segments, 2½" wide.

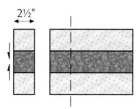

Make 1 strip set, 6½" × 11".
Cut 4 segments, 2½" × 6½".

3 Sew two dark and one light 2½" × 6" rectangle together to make a strip set. Cut the strip set into two segments, 2½" wide.

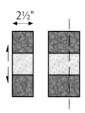

Make 1 strip set, 6" × 6½".
Cut 2 segments, 2½" × 6½".

4 Sew two segments from step 2 and one segment from step 3 together to make a Nine Patch block that measures 6½" square, including seam allowances. Make two matching blocks; then repeat the steps to make a total of 14 blocks.

Make 14 blocks,
6½" × 6½".

Constructing the Quilt

The quilt is assembled in vertical rows of blocks and cream vertical sashing strips. Rows 2, 3, 4, and 5 are each constructed with half blocks at the top or bottom. You'll cut two Anvil blocks and two Sixteen Patch blocks to make half blocks.

1 Choose an Anvil block that you want to cut. Draw a diagonal line, ¼" away from the diagonal center, on the right side of the block. This will later be the cutting line. Sew a line of straight stitches ⅛" inside the drawn line. This line of stitches will be in the seam allowance; it will help to stabilize the bias edges and keep the seams from coming apart after cutting. Using a ruler and rotary cutter, cut on the drawn line. The triangle with the line of stitches is the part that you will use to create the half block. Discard the remainder of the block (the smaller triangle). Repeat to cut a second Anvil block.

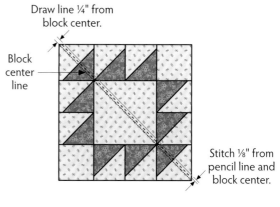

Draw line ¼" from block center.

Block center line

Stitch ⅛" from pencil line and block center.

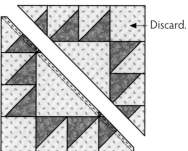

Discard.

2 Arrange and sew seven Anvil blocks, one half block, 14 large red setting triangles, and two large red corner triangles together to create a vertical row. Make two rows. The rows should measure 85⅜" long.

Make 2 rows,
11⅞" × 85⅜".

3 Repeat step 1 to cut two Sixteen Patch blocks in half.

4 Arrange and sew seven Sixteen Patch blocks, one half block, 14 large red setting triangles, and two large red corner triangles together to create a vertical row. Make two rows that measure 85⅜" long.

Make 2 rows,
11⅞" × 85⅜".

5 Arrange and sew seven Nine Patch blocks, three Star blocks, 18 small red setting triangles, and four small red corner triangles together to create a vertical row. Make two rows, noting the different block placement in each row. The rows should measure 85⅜" long.

Make 1 of each row,
9" × 85⅜".

6 Referring to the quilt assembly diagram, arrange and sew the rows together with the four cream 3½" × 85⅜" sashing strips. Sew a cream 4½" × 85⅜" border strip to each side to complete the quilt top, which should measure approximately 83" × 85⅜".

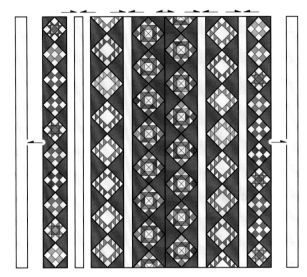

Quilt assembly

Finishing the Quilt

For help with any of the finishing steps, go to ShopMartingale.com/HowtoQuilt.

1 Layer the quilt top with the batting and backing. Quilt by hand or machine. The quilt shown is quilted with parallel lines or a feathered design in the setting triangles, a diagonal grid in the sashing and border, a floral design in the Anvil and Sixteen Patch blocks, and arcs in the Star and Nine Patch blocks.

2 Make the binding using the 1⅞"-wide strips and attach it to the quilt.

THE QUILTING BEE

Quilting bees have existed since colonial times. Whether you're sitting around a quilting frame and stitching on someone's quilt or meeting at your local quilt shop with a group of like-minded friends, a quilting bee is a chance to socialize, chat, gossip, and share secrets and dreams. Both Grandma Moses and Morgan Weistling have depicted quilting bees in their paintings.

Today's bees are often smaller local groups from a larger guild, and block exchanges can be one activity of the bee. For a block exchange to work properly, the group must decide on guidelines and ensure that all the exchangers follow these rules. The group decides on a quilt they would like to make and chooses a leader, and then the math begins: what size will the finished quilt be, how many blocks are needed, how many participants will there be, and finally how many blocks will each participant need to make. The group selects fabrics and a deadline.

The quilt that you see here is the result of one exchange. Our group is not part of a typical bee, but instead a group that meets four or five times a year at a quilt retreat held at Camp Blanding, an Air National Guard Training Center, in Starke, Florida. This was our Churn Dash exchange, and we had 12 participants: Paula Barnes, Mary Ellen Robison, Gloria Parsons, Vicky Iannucci, Phyllis Anderson, Wynette Browning, Diane Webber, Donna Brantley, Pat Meeks, Sara Higginbotham, Ronda Stockton, and Lynn Rogers.

Paula was our leader, so she provided us with a handout that included all of the necessary details: the needed numbers of light Churn Dash blocks, dark Churn Dash blocks, and half-square-triangle units, as well as yardage requirements, recommended fabrics, and a diagram of a possible layout for our finished blocks. We had a year to complete our blocks, but of course many of us procrastinated, resulting in comical emails and texts between the group as we scrambled to meet the deadline.

Many of us finished our quilts, laying out the blocks in a number of different settings. The Quilting Bee quilt shown is Paula's design.

Postcard of the Thirty-First Division Headquarters, Camp Blanding, Florida.
BOSTON PUBLIC LIBRARY

THE QUILTING BEE

FINISHED QUILT 91½" × 91½" ◆ **FINISHED BLOCK** 5" × 5"

Designed and assembled by Paula Barnes; blocks pieced by block-exchange group members; top pieced by Mary Ellen Robison; quilted by Cathy Peters of Palm Tree Quilting and Mary Ellen Robison

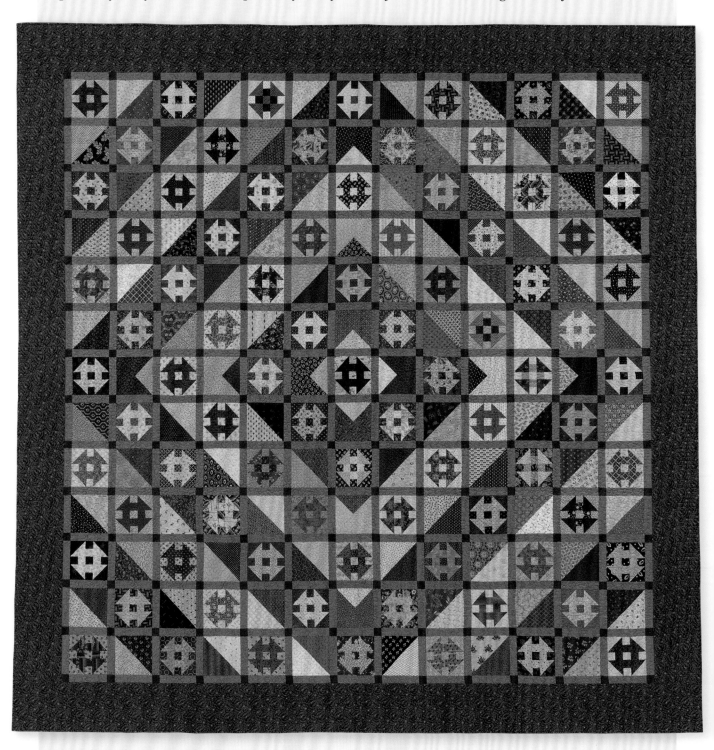

Materials

Yardage is based on 42"-wide fabric; fat eighths measure 9" × 21".

- 44 fat eighths of assorted light prints for blocks
- 44 fat eighths of assorted dark prints for blocks
- 2⅜ yards of tan print for sashing
- ½ yard of brown print for sashing cornerstones
- 2¾ yards of charcoal print for border*
- ¾ yard of fabric for binding
- 8½ yards of fabric for backing
- 100" × 100" piece of batting
- 2" finished Star Singles papers (optional)**

*If you want to use the same charcoal print for binding, you'll need 3⅜ yards.

**See "Using Star Singles" below right before cutting.

Cutting

Carefully label the triangles (size and block name) and other pieces when cutting to stay organized and avoid confusion when piecing the blocks.

SETTING BLOCKS

From *each of 4* of the assorted dark prints, cut:
1 square, 6¾" × 6¾"; cut into quarters diagonally to make 4 triangles (16 total; 4 are extra)
1 square, 6¼" × 6¼"; cut in half diagonally to make 2 triangles (8 total)

From *each of 36* of the assorted dark prints, cut:
1 square, 6¼" × 6¼"; cut in half diagonally to make 2 triangles (72 total)

From *each of 2* of the assorted light prints, cut:
2 squares, 6¾" × 6¾"; cut into quarters diagonally to make 8 triangles (16 total; 4 are extra)
1 square, 6¼" × 6¼"; cut in half diagonally to make 2 (4 total)

From *each of 36* of the assorted light prints, cut:
1 square, 6¼" × 6¼"; cut in half diagonally to make 2 triangles (72 total)

CHURN DASH BLOCKS

From *each* of the 44 assorted dark prints, cut:
4 squares, 3¼" × 3¼" (176 total)
2 strips, 1½" × 7" (88 total)
1 square, 1½" × 1½" (44 total)

From *each* of the 44 assorted light prints, cut:
4 squares, 3¼" × 3¼" (176 total)
2 strips, 1½" × 7" (88 total)
1 square, 1½" × 1½" (44 total)

SASHINGS AND BORDER

From the tan print, cut:
52 strips, 1½" × 42"; crosscut into 364 rectangles, 1½" × 5½"

From brown print, cut:
8 strips, 1½" × 42"; crosscut into 196 squares, 1½" × 1½"

From the charcoal print, cut on the *lengthwise* grain:
2 strips, 6½" × 79½"
2 strips, 6½" × 91½"

From the binding fabric, cut:
10 strips, 1⅞" × 42"

USING STAR SINGLES

If you want to use 2" finished Star Singles papers, do not cut the 3¼" squares. Instead, skip step 1 of "Making the Setting Blocks" on page 42 and follow the directions on the package to cut the following pieces.

From *each* of the 44 assorted dark prints, cut:
1 square, 6½" × 6½" (44 total)

From *each* of the 44 assorted light prints, cut:
1 square, 6½" × 6½" (44 total)

Making the Setting Blocks

Press the seam allowances as indicated by the arrows in the illustrations.

1 Sew a dark and a light 6¼" triangle together to make setting block A. Press and trim to 5½" square. Make 72 of setting block A.

 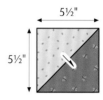

Setting block A.
Make 72.

2 Sew a dark and a light 6¾" triangle together as shown. Add a matching light 6¼" triangle, centering it on the pieced triangle. The triangles are cut oversized and will not match at this point. Don't worry; they'll be trimmed in steps 4 and 5. Make four of setting block B.

Make 4 units.

Setting block B.
Make 4.

3 Sew a light and dark 6¾" triangle together as shown, making a mirror image of the step 2 unit. Add a matching dark 6¼" triangle, centering it as before. Make eight of setting block C.

Make 8 units.

Setting block C.
Make 8.

4 Align the 45° line of a square ruler with the diagonal seam line of a block B as shown, making sure the 2¾" lines meet in the center of the block. Make sure the 5½" lines on the ruler meet on the diagonal seam line. The 5½" line should also align with the diagonal seam along the edge of the block. Trim along the top and right edges of the ruler.

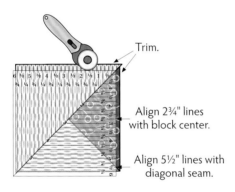

Trim.

Align 2¾" lines with block center.

Align 5½" lines with diagonal seam.

ANOTHER EXCHANGE OPTION

Instead of a block exchange with your group, try a fabric exchange. Pick a theme, and then decide on the size of the fabric (anything from strips to fat quarters), the number of participants, and the number of fabrics each participant will bring. Follow up a year later with a show-and-tell of quilts made from the exchange.

5 Rotate the block 180° so that you can trim the other sides. Align the 45° line of the ruler with the diagonal seam line of the block, making sure the 2¾" lines meet in the center. The 5½" lines on the ruler should align with the previously cut edges. Trim along the top and right sides of the square ruler. Repeat the trimming steps for each of the four B blocks and eight C blocks.

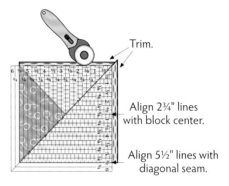

Trim.

Align 2¾" lines with block center.

Align 5½" lines with diagonal seam.

Making the Churn Dash Blocks

You'll make the Churn Dash blocks in pairs, one with a light background and one with a dark background. After you make several pairs, feel free to make units and cut strip-set segments for several blocks before sewing them together. You can then mix and match the units to make scrappy blocks as in a few of the blocks in Paula's quilt.

1 Referring to "Half-Square-Triangle Units" on page 92, mark four matching light 3¼" squares and layer them right sides together with four matching dark 3¼" squares. Sew, cut, press, and then trim to 2½" square. Make eight half-square-triangle units.

2½"

2½"

Make 8 units.

2   Sew a matching dark 1½" × 7" strip and a matching light 1½" × 7" strip together as shown to make a strip set. Make two matching strip sets; crosscut into eight segments that measure 1½" wide.

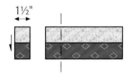

Make 2 strip sets, 2½" × 7".
Cut 8 segments, 1½" × 2½".

3   Arrange and sew four half-square-triangle units from step 1, four segments from step 2, and one matching dark 1½" square together into three rows as shown. Press and sew the rows together to make Churn Dash A block. The block should measure 5½" square, including seam allowances. Make 44 total.

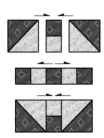

Block A.
Make 44 blocks,
5½" × 5½".

4   Repeat step 3 with a matching light 1½" square to make Churn Dash block B.

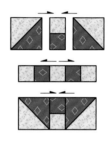
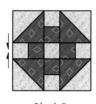

Block B.
Make 1 block,
5½" × 5½".

5   Repeat steps 1–4 to make a total of 44 of each Churn Dash block. Three of the Churn Dash B blocks are extra; only 41 will be used.

Block A.
Make 44 blocks,
5½" × 5½".

Block B.
Make 44 blocks,
5½" × 5½".

Constructing the Quilt

1 Sew 13 tan 1½" × 5½" sashing rectangles and 14 brown 1½" cornerstone squares together into a row. Press. Make 14 rows.

2 Referring to the quilt assembly diagram below, lay out the Churn Dash blocks, alternate blocks, and tan 1½" × 5½" sashing rectangles in 13 horizontal rows. Place a sashing row between each block row and along the top and bottom. Make sure that all of the alternate blocks are in the correct position and oriented correctly. Sew the blocks into rows.

3 Sew the rows together to complete the quilt center. It should measure 79½" square, including seam allowances.

4 Sew the charcoal 6½" × 79½" strips to the sides of the quilt and press. Sew the charcoal print 6½" × 91½" strips to the top and bottom to complete the quilt top. It should measure 91½" square.

Finishing the Quilt

For help with any of the finishing steps, go to ShopMartingale.com/HowtoQuilt.

1 Layer the quilt top with the batting and backing. Quilt by hand or machine. The quilt shown is machine quilted in an overall meandering design.

2 Make the binding using the 1⅞"-wide strips and attach it to the quilt.

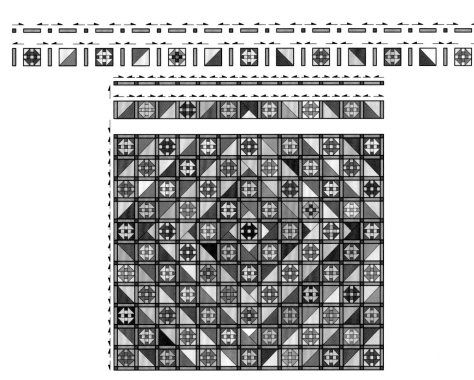

Quilt assembly

MARY'S QUILT

Born on May 22, 1844, in Allegheny, Pennsylvania, Mary Cassatt was one of the leading artists in the Impressionist movement. Raised in an affluent family, Mary traveled abroad with her family and was raised to be a proper wife and mother. Although women of her social status were discouraged from pursuing careers, Mary enrolled in the Pennsylvania Academy of the Fine Arts at the age of 16. Unfortunately, she found the curriculum to be lacking and the male faculty and students resentful of her attendance. Against her father's wishes, Mary decided to leave the Academy and move to Paris, where she could study the Old Masters on her own. She studied at the Louvre, and in 1868, one of her portraits was selected for exhibition by the prestigious Paris Salon.

With the outbreak of the Franco-Prussian War in 1870, Mary was forced to return home, where the artistic freedom she enjoyed in Paris was gone, as well as any financial support for her painting. In need of money, Mary sold some of her paintings to a dealer in Chicago, but they were lost in the Great Fire of 1871.

Mary returned to Europe to work on paintings commissioned by the Archbishop of Pittsburgh and eventually returned to Paris to settle there permanently. She began to experiment artistically and gained the interest and encouragement of prominent Impressionist Edgar Degas. Their friendship grew, and through his support, Mary exhibited eleven of her paintings with the Impressionists in 1878.

While Impressionists are most known for their landscapes, Mary Cassatt is famous for her portraits, especially those of women in everyday settings and those of mothers and children. Her style was still evolving even through her last Impressionist exhibit in 1886.

Mary's failing health and the untimely death of her brother left her without a desire to paint. In 1915, blindness caused by diabetes forced her to stop painting completely. Mary died in France on June 14, 1926, having spent the last 11 years in almost total blindness and unable to enjoy her painting.

Mary Cassatt, 1914.
WIKIMEDIA COMMONS

MARY'S QUILT

FINISHED QUILT 77" × 77" ♦ **FINISHED BLOCK** 6" × 6"
Designed by Paula Barnes; pieced by Paula Barnes and Mary Ellen Robison;
quilted by Marcella Pickett of Crooked Creek Quilts

Materials

Yardage is based on 42"-wide fabric.

- 81 scraps, 9" × 11", of assorted light prints for blocks*
- 81 scraps, 9" × 11", of assorted medium and dark prints for blocks*
- 64 scraps, 7" × 7", of assorted light prints for setting squares
- ⅞ yard of black print for setting triangles**
- ⅝ yard of fabric for binding
- 7 yards of fabric for backing
- 83" × 83" piece of batting

You can also use Layer Cake squares, 10" × 10", if you wish.

**If you want to use the same black print for binding, you'll need 1⅜ yards.*

Cutting

From *each* of the 81 assorted light prints for blocks, cut:
1 square, 3¾" × 3¾" (81 total)
4 squares, 2½" × 2½" (324 total)

From *each* of the 81 assorted medium and dark prints, cut:
2 squares, 3¾" × 3¾" (162 total)
1 square, 2½" × 2½" (81 total)
1 square, 3¾" × 3¾" (81 total)

From *each* of the 64 assorted light prints for setting squares, cut:
1 square, 6½" × 6½" (64 total)

From the black print, cut:
8 squares, 9¾" × 9¾"; cut into quarters diagonally to make 32 side triangles
2 squares, 5⅛" × 5⅛"; cut in half diagonally to make 4 corner triangles

From the binding fabric, cut:
8 strips, 1⅞" × 42"

Making the Blocks

Press the seam allowances as indicated by the arrows in the illustrations.

1 Select one light 3¾" square, one medium or dark 3¾" square, and two matching medium or dark 3¾" squares. With a pencil, draw two diagonal lines on the wrong side of the light 3¾" square and the single 3¾" square, making an *X*. Place each marked square right sides together with one of the matching 3¾" squares. Sew ¼" from both sides of *one* of the pencil lines. Cut apart on the drawn lines and press.

Make 4 of each unit.

2 Sew the units together in pairs to make four identical hourglass units. Trim and square up the hourglass units to 2½" square referring to "Trimming Hourglass Units" on page 35.

Make 4 units.

3 Arrange and sew the four hourglass units, four matching light 2½" squares, and one medium or dark 2½" square together into three rows. Sew the rows together and press to make a block that measures 6½" square, including seam allowances. Make a total of 81 blocks.

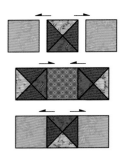 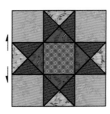

Make 81 blocks, 6½" × 6½".

A HOME FOR SCRAPS

No matter how many scrap quilts you make, scraps never seem to go away. The blocks in this quilt are perfect for paring down your scrap stash. The setting squares offer an opportunity to incorporate favorite light prints and background fabrics, giving them a permanent home.

Constructing the Quilt

Referring to the quilt assembly diagram below, arrange and sew the Star blocks and setting squares together in diagonal rows, adding the side setting triangles to the ends of each row as indicated. Note the layout of the blocks. The lightest Star blocks and setting squares are in the center, and the fabrics get darker as the blocks progress to the edges. Sew the rows together. Add the corner triangles last. The quilt top should measure approximately 77" square.

Finishing the Quilt

For help with any of the finishing steps, go to ShopMartingale.com/HowtoQuilt.

1 Layer the quilt top with the batting and backing. Quilt by hand or machine. The quilt shown is quilted with a floral-like feather design in the alternate blocks and arcs in the pieced blocks.

2 Make the binding using the 1⅞"-wide strips and attach it to the quilt.

Quilt assembly

GARDEN PATH

The Gardens of Monticello are renowned for their beauty. They were originally designed by Thomas Jefferson for his plantation located near Charlottesville, Virginia. The 5,000-acre plantation included a flower garden, a fruit orchard, and a vegetable garden.

Jefferson's interest in gardening dates to 1766 when he began keeping a detailed description in his garden book of the flowers growing around his home in Shadwell, Virginia. He read extensively about gardening but was most influenced by Thomas Whaley's theory of naturalistic gardening. Jefferson also toured English gardens and was especially drawn to the gardens that featured curvilinear paths, informal planting of flowers, unregimented borders, and the use of wildflowers.

Jefferson inherited Monticello in 1757 and eventually moved there in 1770, but it wasn't until 1807 that work on the gardens began. Most of the planting was done between 1808 and 1812 and used plants that Jefferson brought home from his extensive travels as well as plants and seeds provided by family and friends.

The gardens declined after Jefferson's death, but in 1938 the Thomas Jefferson Memorial Foundation contacted the Garden Club of Virginia and requested help with the Gardens of Monticello. Fortunately, they were able to locate Jefferson's garden book, and the gardens were restored to their original glory. Visitors are welcome to stop by and enjoy their beauty.

Monticello, Charlottesville, Virginia.
BILLY HATHORN, WIKIMEDIA COMMONS

GARDEN PATH

FINISHED QUILT 81¾" × 94¼" ◆ **FINISHED BLOCK** 6¼" × 6¼"

Designed by Paula Barnes; pieced by Mary Ellen Robison;
quilted by Marcella Pickett of Crooked Creek Quilts

Materials

Yardage is based on 42"-wide fabric; fat quarters measure 18" × 21".

- 14 fat quarters of assorted dark prints for blocks
- 6⅜ yards of cream print for blocks*
- ¾ yard of fabric for binding
- 8⅝ yards of fabric for backing
- 90" × 103" piece of batting

*If you want to use the same cream print for binding, you'll need 7 yards.

Cutting

Because fat quarters vary in length, do not trim the selvages from the fat quarters or the cream print. Cut carefully, as you'll need all of the 21" of length. If your strips are not at least 21" long, you may need extra strips.

From *each* of the 14 assorted dark prints, cut:
10 strips, 1¾" × 21" (140 total; 8 are extra)*

From the cream print, cut:
49 strips, 1¾" × 42"; cut each strip in half to make
    98 strips, 1¾" × 21"
5 strips, 1¾" × 42"; crosscut into 98 squares,
    1¾" × 1¾"
9 strips, 4¼" × 42"; cut each strip in half to make
    18 strips, 4½" × 21". From *1* of the half strips,
    cut 1 rectangle, 4¼" × 6¾"
11 strips, 6¾" × 42"; crosscut into 96 rectangles,
    4¼" × 6¾"

From the binding fabric, cut:
10 strips, 1⅞" × 42"

*You'll have 8 extra strips, but you may need some or all of them if the strips are not at least 21" long.

ORGANIZING THE PIECES

To stay organized when cutting and piecing, Mary Ellen suggests using four large plastic zip bags, labeled with the block letter and part. Place strips and pieces in them as you cut.

Block A strip sets. Place 7 dark strips, 1¾" × 21", from *each* of the 14 fat quarters (98 total) and 98 cream strips, 1¾" × 21", into this bag.

Block A cream centers. Place 98 cream 1¾" squares into this bag.

Block B strip sets. Place 34 dark strips, 1¾" × 21", and 17 cream strips, 4¼" × 21", in this bag.

Block B centers. Place 97 cream rectangles, 4¼" × 6¾", in this bag.

2 Sew together two of the segments to make a four-patch unit that measures 3" square, including seam allowances. Make 392 scrappy four-patch units.

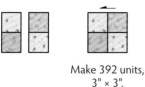

Make 392 units,
3" × 3".

3 Arrange and sew four four-patch units, four segments from step 1, and one cream 1¾" square (from the "block A cream centers" bag) into three rows. Sew the rows together to complete block A, which should measure 6¾" square. Make 98 scrappy A blocks.

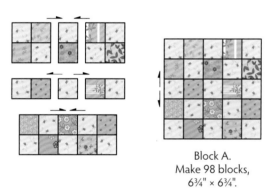

Block A.
Make 98 blocks,
6¾" × 6¾".

Making Block A

Press the seam allowances as indicated by the arrows in the illustrations.

1 Pull a dark and a cream 1¾" × 21" strip from the "block A strip sets" bag. Sew together to make a strip set. Cut the strip set into 12 segments, 1¾" wide. Repeat for the remaining strips in the bag to make a total of 98 strip sets; cut a total of 1,176 segments.

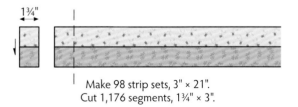

Make 98 strip sets, 3" × 21".
Cut 1,176 segments, 1¾" × 3".

Making Block B

1 Pull two different dark 1¾" × 21" strips and one cream 4¼" × 21" strip from the "block B strip sets" bag. Join to make a strip set. Cut the strip set into 12 segments, 1¾" wide. Repeat with the remaining strips in the bag to make 17 strip sets total; cut 194 segments.

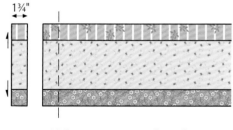

Make 17 strip sets, 6¾" × 21".
Cut 194 segments, 1¾" × 6¾".

2 Sew together two different segments from step 1 with one cream 4¼" × 6¾" rectangle (from the "block B centers" bag) to make block B, which should measure 6¾" square. Make 97 scrappy B blocks.

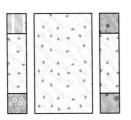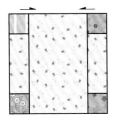

Block B.
Make 97 blocks,
6¾" × 6¾".

Constructing the Quilt

Arrange the blocks into 15 rows of 13 blocks each, alternating the A and B blocks as shown. Sew the blocks into rows and then sew the rows together to complete the quilt top. It should measure 81¾" × 94¼".

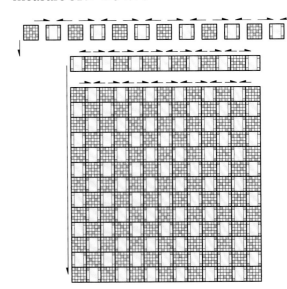

Quilt assembly

Finishing the Quilt

For help with any of the finishing steps, go to ShopMartingale.com/HowtoQuilt.

1 Layer the quilt top with the batting and backing. Quilt by hand or machine. The quilt shown is machine quilted with a feathered wreath in the light open areas and a diagonal grid in the small squares.

2 Make the binding using the 1⅞"-wide strips and attach it to the quilt.

POTATO CHIP STARS

While recipes for potato chips appeared in cookbooks prior to the 1850s, the legend of George Crum, Kate Wicks, and their invention of the potato chip is probably the most interesting. Born in 1824, George was an American chef who honed his culinary skills at Cary Moon's Lake House on Saratoga Lake in upstate New York. Moon's Lake House was an expensive restaurant that catered to the wealthy families from Manhattan that vacationed at their "camps" on the lake.

Kate Wicks was George's sister, and they worked side by side in the kitchen. The story goes that she dropped a thin slice of potato into the pan of fat, fished it out, and set it aside. George tasted it, liked it, and said, "We'll have plenty of these." This was the invention of "Saratoga Chips."

One night, a dinner guest returned his French fries to the kitchen because he felt they were too thick. George decided to annoy the customer by serving him a much thinner fry that he overcooked and over-salted. To his surprise, the guest was ecstatic over the browned, paper-thin potatoes, and the potato chip was born.

In 1860, George opened his own restaurant, called Crum's, in Malta, New York. It's said he served a basket of chips at every table. In 1932, Herman Lay founded Lay's, and his potato chips became the first successfully marketed national brand.

Paula calls the 4" block used in this quilt her "potato chip block" because they're like potato chips—you can't stop after just one!

George Crum

POTATO CHIP STARS

FINISHED QUILT 77" × 77" ◆ **FINISHED BLOCK** 9" × 9"

Designed by Paula Barnes; pieced by Paula Barnes and Mary Ellen Robison;
quilted by Cathy Peters of Palm Tree Quilting

Materials

Yardage is based on 42"-wide fabric.

- ¼ yard *each* of 33 assorted dark prints for blocks
- ¼ yard *each* of 33 assorted light prints for blocks
- 1 yard of brown print for blocks
- 1½ yards of navy print for sashing strips
- 1½ yards of black solid for setting triangles and sashing squares*
- ⅝ yard of fabric for binding
- 7⅛ yards of fabric for backing
- 85" × 85" piece of batting
- 1" finished Star Singles papers (optional)

If you want to use the same black solid for binding, you'll need 2 yards.

**See "Using Star Singles" below right before cutting.*

Cutting

From *each* of the 33 assorted dark prints, cut:
20 squares, 2¼" × 2¼" (660 total)
5 squares, 2½" × 2½" (165 total)

From *each* of the 33 assorted light prints, cut:
20 squares, 2¼" × 2¼" (660 total)
21 squares, 1½" × 1½" (693 total)

From *each of 8* assorted light prints, cut:
1 square, 1½" × 1½" (8 total)

From the brown print, cut:
7 strips, 4½" × 42"; crosscut into 164 rectangles, 1½" × 4½"

From the navy print, cut:
5 strips, 9½" × 42"; crosscut into 100 strips, 2" × 9½"

From the black solid, cut:
4 squares, 16⅛" × 16⅛"; cut into quarters diagonally to make 16 side triangles
2 squares, 9⅜" × 9⅜"; cut in half diagonally to make 4 corner triangles
3 strips, 2" × 42"; crosscut into 60 squares, 2" × 2"

From the binding fabric, cut:
8 strips, 1⅞" × 42"

USING STAR SINGLES

If you use the 1" Star Singles papers, *do not* cut the 2¼" squares. Instead, skip step 1 of "Making the Star Blocks" on page 62 and follow the directions on the package to cut the following pieces.

From *each* of the 33 assorted dark prints, cut:
5 squares, 4½" × 4½" (165 total)

From *each* of the 33 assorted light prints, cut:
5 squares, 4½" × 4½" (165 total)

Making the Star Blocks

Press the seam allowances as indicated by the arrows in the illustrations.

1 Referring to "Half-Square-Triangle Units" on page 92, mark four matching light 2¼" squares and layer them right sides together with four matching dark 2¼" squares. Sew, cut, press, and trim the units to 1½" square. You'll have eight identical half-square-triangle units.

Make 8 units.

2 Sew two half-square-triangle units together to form a star point. Make four star-point units measuring 1½" × 2½".

Make 4 units,
1½" × 2½".

3 Arrange the four star-point units, one dark 2½" square, and four light 1½" squares together into three rows. Use matching light squares or squares from a different light print. Sew the rows and then sew the rows together to complete a star unit that measures 4½" square. Make a total of 165 star units. You'll use 164 in the quilt with one left over to use for a label.

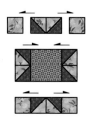

Make 165 units,
4½" × 4½".

LOOKING AHEAD

While you're piecing the blocks, think about how you'll quilt your quilt—or how you would like it to be quilted. Diagonal grids, Baptist fan, feathers, and simple outline or in-the-ditch quilting are all appropriate for quilts that you want to have an old-fashioned appearance.

4 Arrange and sew four star units that have the same background value, four brown 1½" × 4½" rectangles, and one light 1½" square together into three rows. Sew the rows together to complete a block that measures 9½" square. Make a total of 41 blocks.

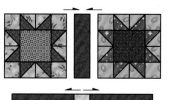

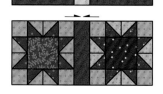

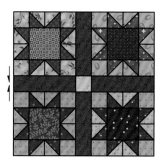

Make 41 blocks,
9½" × 9½".

Constructing the Quilt

Referring to the quilt assembly diagram below, arrange and sew the blocks, navy 2" × 9½" strips, and black 2" squares together in rows. Note the layout of the blocks. The lightest blocks are in the center, and the blocks get progressively darker as they go toward the quilt edges. Add the side setting triangles to the ends of each row and sew the rows together. Add the corner triangles last.

Finishing the Quilt

For help with any of the finishing steps, go to ShopMartingale.com/HowtoQuilt.

1. Layer the quilt top with the batting and backing. Quilt by hand or machine. The quilt shown is machine quilted using a feathered wreath design in the blocks, a cable in the sashing, and a feathered design in the setting triangles.

2. Make the binding using the 1⅞"-wide strips and attach it to the quilt.

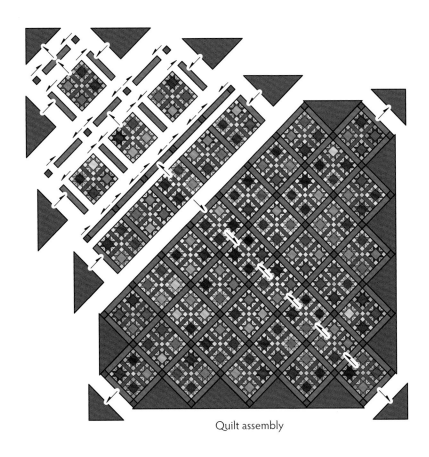

Quilt assembly

KENTUCKY BASKETS

Baskets, baskets, baskets! We see them everywhere, used for every purpose—both functional and decorative. Baskets are made from different materials, they appear in different styles, and many have specific functions. Basketmaking has been a part of our lives for centuries. Traces of baskets were even found in the Egyptian pyramids.

Once men and women learned to weave, baskets became a part of their lives. They were used to carry goods to new places and were often traded and sold, thus introducing styles and techniques from one region to another. The baskets reflected the influence of the people that made them. Some Native American tribes went so far as to weave stories and symbols into their baskets. The shape of a basket was often dictated by its function. For example, the egg basket's form allows for the distribution of the eggs' weight and ensures the eggs arrived safely to market.

Kentucky is well known for the craftsmanship found in its baskets.

Through the influence of Native Americans and the basketmaking heritage that settlers from other areas brought to Kentucky, basketmaking flourished. The settlers learned to use the different materials available to them, particularly white oak because of its abundance. Guilds have since been formed to preserve this history and provide resources for basket makers. Through classes and demos, new and old basketmaking techniques are taught to new basket makers. The Mammoth Cave Basket Makers have even established a museum and demonstrate at the Kentucky Arts and Crafts Juried Show in Louisville.

Handmade white oak baskets in the Hart County/ Mammoth Cave, Kentucky, Tradition. Front row, left to right: *Flower Basket by Ollie Childress, Half Bushel Egg Basket by Lestel Childress.* Back row, left to right: *Kentucky Egg Basket by Lestel Childress, Kentucky Egg Basket with waxed linen trim by Beth Hester, Fan Basket by Lestel Childress.*
SCOTT GILBERT

KENTUCKY BASKETS

FINISHED QUILT 87½" × 96" ◆ **FINISHED BLOCK** 3" × 3"

Designed by Paula Barnes; pieced by Mary Ellen Robison;
quilted by Marcella Pickett of Crooked Creek Quilts

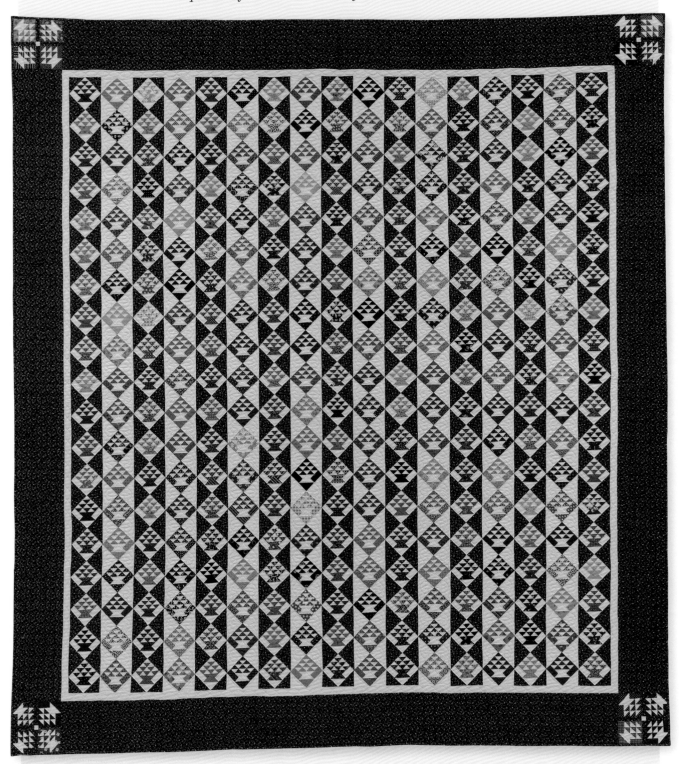

Materials

Yardage is based on 42"-wide fabric.

- 8⅝ yards of tan print for blocks and inner border
- 171 rectangles, 9" × 11" *each*, of assorted dark prints for blocks
- 4¾ yards of navy print for alternate blocks and outer border*
- ¾ yard of fabric for binding
- 8¾ yards of fabric for backing
- 96" × 104" piece of batting
- ¾" finished Primitive Gatherings triangle papers (optional)**
- 3" finished Star Singles papers (optional)

If you want to use the same navy print for binding, you'll need 5⅜ yards.

**See "Using Triangle Papers" at right before cutting fabrics.*

Cutting

From the tan print, cut:

69 strips, 2" × 42"; crosscut into 1,368 squares, 2" × 2"

13 strips, 2¾" × 42"; crosscut into 171 squares, 2¾" × 2¾"

11 strips, 2" × 42"; crosscut into 342 rectangles, 1¼" × 2"

16 strips, 4¼" × 42"; crosscut 144 squares, 4¼" × 4¼"

8 strips, 1½" × 42"

16 squares, 3" × 3", cut in half diagonally to make 32 triangles

4 squares, 1" × 1"

From *each* of the assorted dark prints, cut:

8 squares, 2" × 2" (1,368 total)

1 square, 2¾" × 2¾" (171 total)

2 rectangles, 1¼" × 2" (342 total; 6 are extra)

From the navy print, cut on the *lengthwise* grain:

2 strips, 7" × 85"

2 strips, 7" × 77"

From the remainder of the navy print, cut:

144 squares, 4¼" × 4¼"

9 squares, 5½" × 5½"; cut into quarters diagonally to make 36 side triangles

18 squares, 3" × 3"; cut in half diagonally to make 36 triangles

16 rectangles, 1" × 3½"

From the binding fabric, cut:

10 strips, 1⅞" × 42"

USING TRIANGLE PAPERS

If you want to use triangle papers for the ¾" finished half-square-triangle units in the Basket blocks, you can use ¾" Triangle Paper by Primitive Gatherings. You'll need three packages of 60 sheets. Do not cut the 2" squares. Instead, skip step 1 of "Making the Basket Blocks" on page 68 and follow the directions on the package to cut the following pieces.

From the tan print, cut:
171 squares, 5½" × 5½"

From each assorted dark print, cut:
171 squares, 5½" × 5½"

Use the extra half-square-triangle units to make "Itty Bitty Leftovers" on page 89.

If you use the 3" Star Singles papers, do not cut the 4¼" squares. Instead, skip "Making the Alternate Blocks" on page 69 and follow the directions on the package to cut the following pieces.

From the light print, cut:
36 squares, 8½" × 8½"

From the dark print, cut:
36 squares, 8½" × 8½"

Making the Basket Blocks

Press the seam allowances as indicated by the arrows in the illustrations.

1 Referring to "Half-Square-Triangle Units" on page 92, mark eight tan 2" squares and layer them right sides together with eight matching dark 2" squares. Sew, cut, press, and trim the units to 1¼" square. Make 16 units.

Make 16 units.

2 Repeat step 1 to mark a tan 2¾" square and layer it with a matching dark 2¾" square. Sew, cut, press, and trim the units to 2" square. Make two units.

Make 2 units.

3 Sew six half-square-triangle units from step 1 together into two rows as shown. Sew the rows together to create a unit that measures 2" × 2¾", including seam allowances.

Make 1 unit, 2" × 2¾".

4 Sew two half-square-triangle units from step 1 and one tan 1¼" × 2" rectangle together as shown to create a unit that measures 2" square, including seam allowances.

Make 1 unit, 2" × 2".

5 Arrange and sew a tan 1¼" × 2" rectangle, the unit from step 3, the unit from step 4, and one half-square-triangle unit from step 2 together into two rows. Sew the rows together and press to create a light Basket block that measures 3½" square, including seam allowances.

Make 1 block, 3½" × 3½".

6 Repeat steps 3 and 4 with a matching dark 1¼" × 2" rectangle, positioning the units as shown.

Make 1 unit, 2" × 2¾".   Make 1 unit, 2" × 2".

7 Repeat step 5 with the matching dark 1¼" × 2" rectangle and the remaining half-square-triangle unit from step 2 to create a dark Basket block that measures 3½" square, including seam allowances.

Make 1 block, 3½" × 3½".

8 Repeat steps 1–7 to make a total of 171 light Basket blocks and 168 dark Basket blocks. You'll have extra half-square-triangle units after making the Basket blocks. Use the units in another project. (See "Itty Bitty Leftovers" on page 89.)

Light Basket block.
Make 171 blocks,
3½" × 3½".

Dark Basket block.
Make 168 blocks,
3½" × 3½".

Making the Alternate blocks

Referring to "Half-Square-Triangle Units" on page 92, mark the tan 4¼" squares and layer them right sides together with the navy 4¼" squares. Sew, cut, press, and trim the units to 3½" square. Make 288 blocks.

Make 288 blocks.

Making the Pieced Setting Triangles

1 Sew navy and tan 3" triangles together as shown. Make a total of 16 A triangles and 16 B triangles.

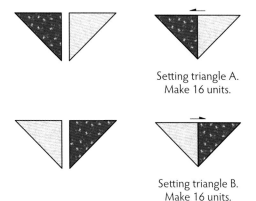

Setting triangle A.
Make 16 units.

Setting triangle B.
Make 16 units.

2 Place the pieced setting triangles aside, keeping each stack labeled or stored in labeled zip bags.

Making the Border Blocks

Arrange and sew four dark Basket blocks, one tan 1" square, and four navy 1" × 3½" sashing rectangles together into three rows as shown. Sew the rows together and press to create a block for the border corner. Make four blocks that measure 7" square, including seam allowances.

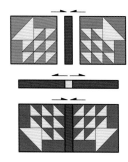 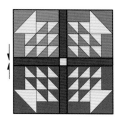

Make 4 blocks,
7" × 7".

Constructing the Quilt

1 Referring to the quilt assembly diagram below, arrange the Basket blocks and alternate blocks in diagonal rows. Pay close attention to the placement and orientation of the blocks. Place a setting triangle and pieced setting triangle at the ends of each row, with the exception of rows 17–19. Sew the blocks into rows and then sew the rows together. Add the corner triangles last. The quilt center should measure approximately 72½" × 81".

2 Measure the length of the quilt through the center. Piece the tan 1½"-wide strips together to make one long strip and cut two strips to the measured length. Sew them to each side of the quilt top.

3 Measure the width of the quilt through the center and repeat step 2 to add tan strips to the top and bottom.

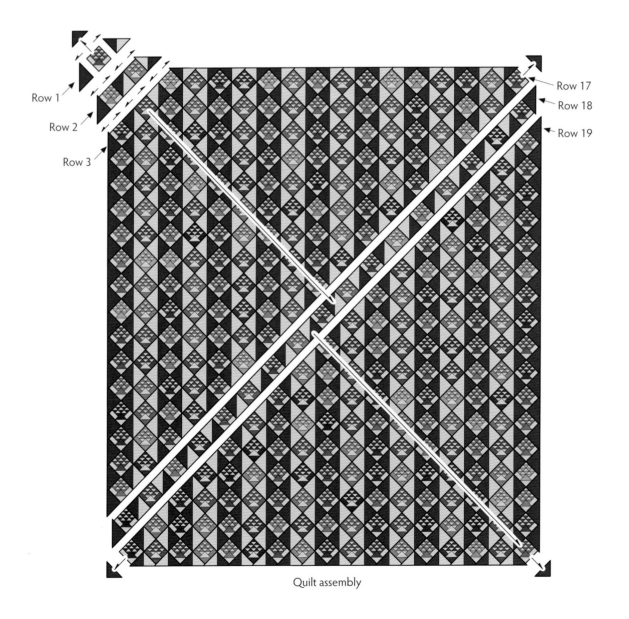

Row 1
Row 2
Row 3

Row 17
Row 18
Row 19

Quilt assembly

4 Measure the length and width of the quilt and trim the navy 7"-wide strips to the measured lengths. Sew the side borders to the quilt.

5 Sew the border blocks to both ends of the remaining border strips and sew them to the top and bottom. The quilt top should measure 87½" × 96".

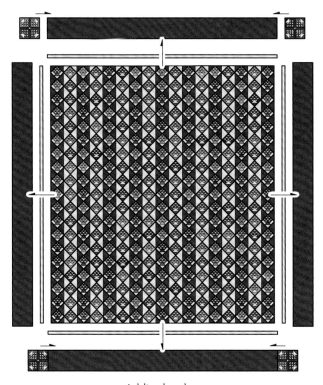

Adding borders

Finishing the Quilt

For help with any of the finishing steps, go to ShopMartingale.com/HowtoQuilt.

1 Layer the quilt top with the batting and backing. Quilt by hand or machine. The quilt shown is machine quilted with a feather design in the alternate blocks. The Basket blocks are outline quilted.

2 Make the binding using the 1⅞"-wide strips and attach it to the quilt.

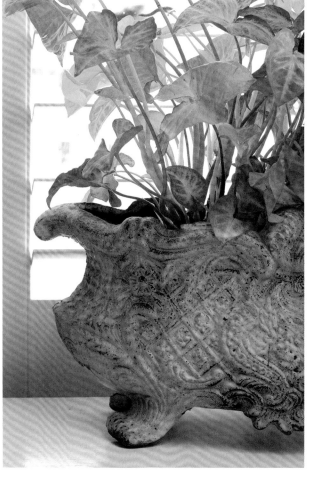

A HOUSE DIVIDED

In a speech on June 16, 1858, at the Illinois Republican State Convention, Abraham Lincoln accepted the nomination as their candidate for US senator and then spoke the now famous quote, "A house divided against itself cannot stand." Lincoln lost that election to Stephen A. Douglas, but the speech most likely launched his campaign and election to the presidency.

The speech, considered one of Lincoln's best, was in response to the US Supreme Court decision regarding Dred Scott, a slave who sued to obtain his freedom. The court ruled that slaves were not citizens of the United States and therefore had no right to sue in federal court. Dred Scott and his wife were bought by a friend of Dred's former master and were later granted their freedom.

With this speech, Lincoln hoped to establish himself as different from Douglas. Lincoln's friends considered it too radical, and his partner, William H. Herndon, suggested that he not give the speech.

Douglas believed in popular sovereignty, the idea that each new state entering the Union would decide if it was to be a free state or a slave state. Lincoln believed that the Union as "a house divided" would not survive this division. The country would have to decide one way or the other—free or slave.

Leonard Swett said the speech defeated Lincoln in his Senate campaign. Swett later wrote, "Nothing could have been more unfortunate or inappropriate; it was saying first the wrong thing, yet he saw it was an abstract truth, but standing by the speech would ultimately find him in the right place."

Dred Scott, circa 1857.
WIKIMEDIA COMMONS

A HOUSE DIVIDED

FINISHED QUILT 92¼" × 92¼" ◆ **FINISHED BLOCK** 5" × 5"
Designed by Paula Barnes; pieced by Mary Ellen Robison;
machine quilted by Sharon Dixon

Materials

Yardage is based on 42"-wide fabric.

- 90 scraps, at least 7" × 7" *each*, of assorted light prints for blocks
- 90 scraps, at least 7" × 7" *each*, of assorted dark prints for blocks
- 1½ yards of cream print for sashing
- 4¾ yards of black print for sashing and border*
- ¾ yard of fabric for binding
- 8½ yards of fabric for backing
- 101" × 101" piece of batting

*If you want to use the same black print for binding, you'll need 5⅜ yards.

ORGANIZING THE PIECES

To stay organized when cutting and piecing, Mary Ellen suggests using three large plastic zip bags, labeled as follows.

Pieced setting triangles. Place 32 two light and 32 dark 4½" triangles in this bag.

Corner triangles. Place the remaining two light and two dark 4½" triangles in this bag.

Scrappy blocks. Place the leftover pieces from step 3 (page 76) in this bag.

Cutting

From *each of 73* of the assorted light prints, cut:
1 square, 6½" × 6½" (73 total)

From *each of 73* of the assorted dark prints, cut:
1 square, 6½" × 6½" (73 total)

From *each of 17* of the assorted light prints, cut:
1 square, 4½" × 4½"; cut in half diagonally to make 2 triangles (34 total)

From *each of 17* of the assorted dark prints, cut:
1 square, 4½" × 4½"; cut in half diagonally to make 2 triangles (34 total)

From the cream print, cut:
9 strips, 5½" × 42"; crosscut into 162 rectangles, 2" × 5½"

From the black print, cut:
29 strips, 2" × 42"

From the remainder of the black print, cut on the *lengthwise* grain:
2 strips, 5" × 86"
2 strips, 5" × 96"

From the binding fabric, cut:
10 strips, 1⅞" × 42"

Making the Hourglass Blocks

Press the seam allowances as indicated by the arrows in the illustrations.

1 Select a light and a dark 6½" square to make a block. With a pencil, draw two diagonal lines on the wrong side of the light square, making an *X*.

2 Place the marked square on the dark square with right sides together. Sew ¼" from both sides of *one* of the pencil lines. Cut apart on both drawn lines and press.

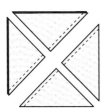

3 Sew two of the units together to create an Hourglass block. Set the remaining two triangle units aside or in the "scrappy blocks" zip bag to be pieced later. Referring to "Trimming Hourglass Units" on page 35, trim and square up the block to measure 5½" square, placing the 2¾" lines at the block center. Repeat the steps to make a total of 73 Hourglass blocks with two colors.

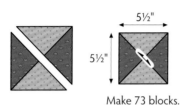

Make 73 blocks.

4 Repeat step 3 using the pieced triangle units from the "scrappy blocks" bag. Make a total of 73 scrappy Hourglass blocks and trim each to 5½" square.

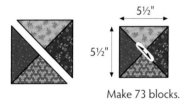

Make 73 blocks.

Making the Pieced Setting Triangles

Sew a light and a dark triangle from the bag labeled "pieced setting triangles" together as shown to make a setting triangle. Make a total of 16 pieced setting triangles with the darker triangle on the left and 16 with the darker triangle on the right.

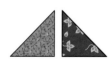

Make 16 units.

Make 16 units.

Constructing the Quilt

1 Referring to the quilt assembly diagram on page 77, arrange the blocks in diagonal rows with the cream 2" × 5½" sashing rectangles and pieced setting triangles. Use a design wall or the floor. Place the darker triangles in the blocks adjacent to the light sashing rectangles. Note that you'll have one extra block.

2 Sew the blocks and cream sashing rectangles into rows. Add a pieced setting triangle to each end and replace the rows in the layout, leaving space for the black sashing strips.

3 Trim the selvage ends from the black 2" × 42" sashing strips and piece them together as needed. Place the sashing strips between each row, trimming them approximately 2" longer on each end than the rows that they will be attached to. You'll trim the ends of the sashing strips to fit the quilt after the center of the quilt has been completed.

4 On the wrong side of the black sashing fabric, use a pencil and ruler to mark a line across the sashing at the beginning and ending of each block. Pin the next row to the sashing, matching the marked lines. This will ensure that your rows line up properly.

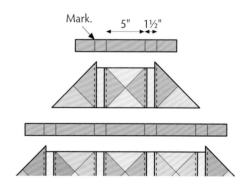

Mark. 5" 1½"

5 Sew the rows and sashing strips together.

6 Trim the excess sashing even with the rest of the quilt. Add the corner triangles to complete the quilt center.

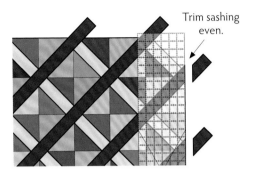

Trim sashing even.

7 Measure the length of the quilt through the center. Cut the black 5" × 86" border strips to that length. Sew them to the sides of the quilt.

8 Measure the width of the quilt through the center, including the borders just added, and cut the black 5" × 96" border strips to that length. Sew them to the top and bottom of the quilt. The quilt top should measure approximately 92¼" square.

Finishing the Quilt

For help with any of the finishing steps, go to ShopMartingale.com/HowtoQuilt.

1 Layer the quilt top with the batting and backing. Quilt by hand or machine. The quilt shown is machine quilted with an overall feather design.

2 Make the binding using the 1⅞"-wide strips and attach it to the quilt.

Quilt assembly

SMITHSON'S LEGACY

James Smithson was an English chemist and mineralogist who was born in 1765. He traveled extensively, kept accurate records of his experiments and collections, and eventually published 27 scientific papers. Smithson was determined to make a name for himself among scientists and was accepted as a member of the Royal Society of London in 1787.

Smithson died on June 27, 1829, in Genoa, Italy, and was buried there in a British cemetery. He never married and left most of his wealth to his nephew, Henry James Hungerford, with the stipulation that should Henry die without an heir, the money would go "to the United States of America, to found at Washington, under the name of the Smithsonian Institution, an Establishment for the increase and diffusion of knowledge among man." Hungerford died on June 5, 1835, leaving no heir, and then began the eight-year congressional debate on how to use the money to meet Smithson's mandate "for the increase and diffusion of knowledge."

In 1838, Attorney Richard Rush traveled to England to claim the bequest for the United States. He returned home with eleven boxes of gold sovereigns, approximately $500,000, plus Smithson's personal items, notes, mineral collections, and library.

Construction began on the Smithsonian Institution, or "the Castle," in 1849, and the building opened in 1855. The Smithsonian Institution is often called the nation's attic. It houses over 150 million items and includes 19 museums, nine research centers, and a zoo, which are mostly located in Washington, DC. In January 1904, Alexander Graham Bell traveled to Genoa to exhume Smithson's body. It was entombed at the Smithsonian in 1905, where it remains today.

The question remains, though, why did James Smithson make this unusual bequest to the United States? For all his travels, he never once visited the United States. His personal papers have been lost, so likely we'll never know what his reasons were.

The Smithsonian Institution Building (the Castle).
WIKIMEDIA COMMONS

SMITHSON'S LEGACY

FINISHED QUILT 68⅜" × 68⅜" ◆ **FINISHED BLOCK** 12" × 12"

Designed by Paula Barnes; pieced by Mary Ellen Robison;
quilted by Marcella Pickett of Crooked Creek Quilts

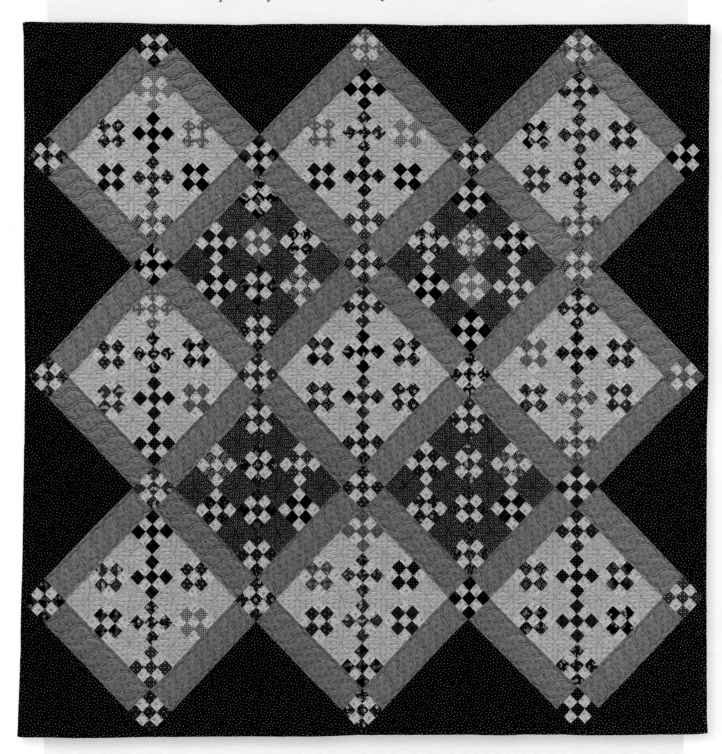

Materials

Yardage is based on 42"-wide fabric.

- 26 scraps, 6" × 13" *each*, of assorted dark prints for nine-patch units
- 1¼ yards of cream print for nine-patch units
- ⅞ yard of light gray print for alternate squares
- ⅜ yard of blue print for alternate squares
- 1⅓ yards of taupe print for sashing
- 1⅜ yards of navy print for setting triangles*
- ⅝ yard of fabric for binding
- 4¼ yards of fabric for backing
- 75" × 75" piece of batting

If you want to use the same navy print for binding, you'll need 1⅞ yards.

Cutting

From *each* of the 26 assorted dark prints, cut:
3 strips, 1½" × 13" (78 total)

From the cream print, cut:
26 strips, 1½" × 42"; crosscut into 78 strips, 1½" × 13"

From the light gray print, cut:
7 strips, 3½" × 42"; crosscut into 72 squares, 3½" × 3½"

From the blue print, cut:
3 strips, 3½" × 42"; crosscut into 32 squares, 3½" × 3½"

From the taupe print, cut:
12 strips, 3½" × 42"; crosscut into 36 rectangles, 3½" × 12½"

From the navy print, cut:
2 squares, 22½" × 22½"; cut into quarters diagonally to make 8 triangles
2 squares, 13⅝" × 13⅝"; cut in half diagonally to make 4 triangles

From the binding fabric, cut:
8 strips, 1⅞" × 42"

Making the Blocks

Press the seam allowances as indicated by the arrows in the illustrations.

1 Select three cream 1½" × 13" strips and three matching dark 1½" × 13" strips.

2 Sew one dark and two cream 1½" × 13" strips together to make a strip set. Cut into seven segments, 1½" wide.

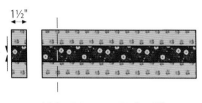

Make 1 strip set, 3½" × 13".
Cut 7 segments, 1½" × 3½".

3 Sew one cream and two matching dark 1½" × 13" strips together. Cut into eight segments, 1½" wide.

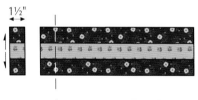

Make 1 strip set, 3½" × 13".
Cut 8 segments, 1½" × 3½".

4 Sew two segments from step 2 and one segment from step 3 together as shown to make a nine-patch unit that measures 3½" square, including seam allowances. Make two units.

Make 2 units,
3½" × 3½".

5 Sew one unit from step 1 and two units from step 2 together as shown to make a nine-patch unit that measures 3½" square, including seam allowances. Make three units.

Make 3 units,
3½" × 3½".

6 Repeat the steps to make a total of 52 light-corner nine-patch units and 78 dark-corner nine-patch units. Two of the dark-corner units will be extra.

Make 52 units,   Make 78 units,
3½" × 3½".   3½" × 3½".

7 Sew four light-corner units, four dark-corner units, and eight light gray 3½" squares together in four rows. Press. Sew the rows together and press to make a block that measures 12½" square, including seam allowances. Make a total of nine blocks.

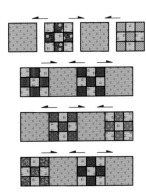 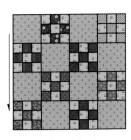

Make 9 blocks,
12½" × 12½".

8 Repeat step 7 using eight blue 3½" squares. Make four blocks.

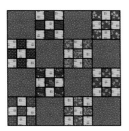

Make 4 blocks,
12½" × 12½".

Constructing the Quilt

Referring to the quilt assembly diagram below, arrange the blocks, nine-patch units, and taupe 3½" × 12½" sashing rectangles together in diagonal rows. Sew the blocks and sashing together to create rows. Then sew the sashing rectangles and nine-patch units together to make sashing rows. Sew a block row together with a sashing row before adding the navy side triangles. Sew the rows together. Add the navy corner triangles last.

Finishing the Quilt

For help with any of the finishing steps, go to ShopMartingale.com/HowtoQuilt.

1 Layer the quilt top with the batting and backing. Quilt by hand or machine. The quilt shown is machine quilted with arcs in the nine-patch units, a fleur-de-lis design in the alternate squares, a twisted cable in the sashing, and a partial wreath design in the setting triangles.

2 Make the binding using the 1⅞"-wide strips and attach it to the quilt.

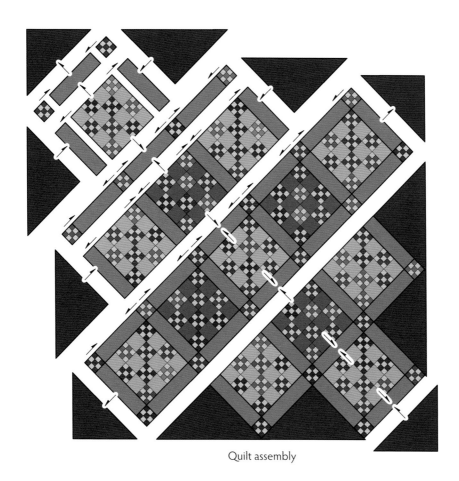

Quilt assembly

PIONEER LIFE

When President Abraham Lincoln signed the Homestead Act of 1862, he created the westward movement, one of the largest migrations of people in the country's history. Pioneers spent up to a year preparing for their trip West. Everything for their journey and eventual settlement on their new land would need to be gathered and packed in a wagon: tools, farm equipment, weapons, dishes, clothing, utensils, books, furniture, bedding, and food. It was suggested for bedding that each person have two to three blankets or quilts, so the women sewed before they left on their trip. The quilts served as memories for these women. Perhaps friends helped to stitch them or even donated fabric for them.

We like to romanticize the pioneer women's journey and imagine them quietly piecing blocks and quilts as they traveled in their covered wagons. In reality, these women walked alongside their wagons all day, and after setting up camp in the evenings and cooking, they most likely didn't have the time or energy to stitch. It was when they were settled and perhaps in need of an additional quilt that they looked at any fabric they could reuse or repurpose. The women pieced scraps of fabric together into blocks and then into quilt tops, often using a block-style technique that focused on geometric shapes (rectangles, squares, and triangles). These shapes would make the most efficient use of their scraps and their time.

These blocks represent the pioneer woman's journey. Blocks were named for these experiences, and when shared, the blocks may receive a new name, one that represents the new quilter's life. Broken Dishes is one such block. Examples of this block date back to the 1790s. Old Tippecanoe, Bow Ties, Hourglass, Whirling Blade, and Yankee Puzzle are all names for this quilt block consisting of four half-square-triangle units in a four-patch square. It's a block that's easy to piece and looks good in scrappy fabrics or striking in just two colors.

A family with their covered wagon, 1886, Loup Valley, Nebraska.
NATIONAL ARCHIVES AND RECORDS ADMINISTRATION

PIONEER LIFE

FINISHED QUILT 43½" × 43½" ◆ **FINISHED BLOCK** 2½" × 2½"

Designed by Paula Barnes; pieced and quilted by Pat Meeks

Materials

Yardage is based on 42"-wide fabric.

- 1¾ yards of cream print for blocks, setting squares, and borders
- 1⅝ yards of navy print for blocks and borders*
- ⅜ yard of fabric for binding
- 2⅞ yards of fabric for backing
- 50" × 50" piece of batting
- 1¼" finished Star Singles papers (optional)**

If you want to use the same navy print for binding, you'll need 1⅞ yards.

**See "Using Star Singles" at right before cutting.*

Cutting

From the cream print, cut:
11 strips, 2½" × 42"; crosscut into 170 squares, 2½" × 2½"
5 strips, 3" × 42"; crosscut into 60 squares, 3" × 3"
8 strips, 1¾" × 42"; crosscut into:
    2 strips, 1¾" × 28"
    2 strips, 1¾" × 30½"
    2 strips, 1¾" × 33"
    2 strips, 1¾" × 35½"
    4 squares, 1¾" × 1¾"

From the navy print, cut on the *lengthwise* grain:
2 strips, 4½" × 35½"
2 strips, 4½" × 43½"

From the remainder of the navy print, cut:
170 squares, 2½" × 2½"

From the binding fabric, cut:
5 strips, 1⅞" × 42"

Making the Blocks

Press the seam allowances as indicated by the arrows in the illustrations.

1 Referring to "Half-Square-Triangle Units" on page 92, mark the cream 2½" squares and layer them right sides together with the navy 2½" squares. Sew, cut, press, and trim the units to 1¾" square. Make 340 half-square-triangle units for the blocks and pieced border.

Make 340 units.

2 Arrange and sew four half-square-triangle units together as shown. The block should measure 3" square. Make 61 blocks.

Make 61 blocks, 3" × 3".

Constructing the Pieced Border

Sew 24 half-square-triangle units together as shown to make a pieced border that measures 1¾" × 30½", including seam allowances. Make four border strips. Sew a cream 1¾" square to both ends of two of the borders.

Make 2 top/bottom borders,
1¾" × 30½".

Make 2 side borders,
1¾" × 33".

Constructing the Quilt

1 Referring to the quilt assembly diagram below, arrange the blocks and cream 3" alternate squares together in 11 rows of 11 blocks each. Sew the blocks into rows and then sew the rows together. The quilt center should measure 28" square, including seam allowances.

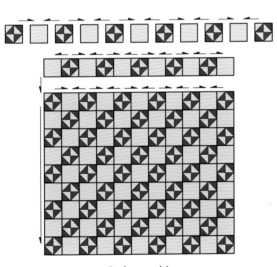

Quilt assembly

2 Sew the cream 1¾" × 28" strips to the sides of the quilt. Sew the cream 1¾" × 30½" strips to the top and bottom.

3 Sew the pieced borders without corner squares to the top and bottom of the quilt, making sure that the dark triangles are adjacent to the first border. Sew the pieced borders with corner squares to the sides. The quilt center should measure 33" square.

4 Sew the cream 1¾" × 33" strips to the sides of the quilt center and the 1¾" × 35½" strips to the top and bottom.

5 Sew the navy 4½" × 35½" strips to the sides of the quilt center and the 4½" × 43½" strips to the top and bottom. The quilt top should measure 43½" square.

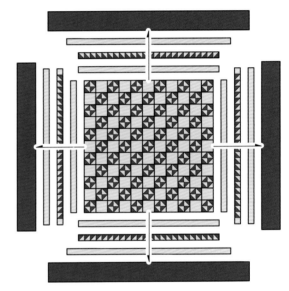

Adding borders

Finishing the Quilt

For help with any of the finishing steps, go to ShopMartingale.com/HowtoQuilt.

1 Layer the quilt top with the batting and backing. Quilt by hand or machine. The quilt shown is machine quilted in an overall meandering design.

2 Make the binding using the 1⅞"-wide strips and attach it to the quilt.

ITTY BITTY LEFTOVERS

This is a smaller version of Pioneer Life on page 84, made with scraps or leftover units from Kentucky Baskets (page 64).

FINISHED QUILT 26½" × 26½" ◆ **FINISHED BLOCK** 1½" × 1½"
Designed by Paula Barnes; pieced by Mary Ellen Robison; quilted by Pat Meeks

Materials

Yardage is based on 42"-wide fabric.

- 170 squares, 2" × 2", of assorted prints for blocks*
- 1 yard of tan print for blocks and borders
- ½ yard of red print for outer border**
- ¼ yard of fabric for binding
- 1 yard of fabric for backing
- 31" × 31" piece of batting

*You won't need these if using leftover half-square-triangle units from Kentucky Baskets.

**If you want to use the same red print for binding, you'll need ⅝ yard.

Cutting

From the tan print, cut:
12 strips, 2" × 42"; crosscut into 230 squares, 2" × 2" (or 3 strips crosscut into 60 squares if using leftover units)
5 strips, 1¼" × 42"; crosscut into:
 2 strips, 1¼" × 17", for border #1
 2 strips, 1¼" × 18½", for border #1
 2 strips, 1¼" × 20", for border #3
 2 strips, 1¼" × 21½", for border #3
 4 squares, 1¼" × 1¼", for pieced border #2

From the red print, cut:
2 strips, 3" × 21½", for border #4
2 strips, 3" × 26½", for border #4

From the binding fabric, cut:
3 strips, 1⅞" × 42"

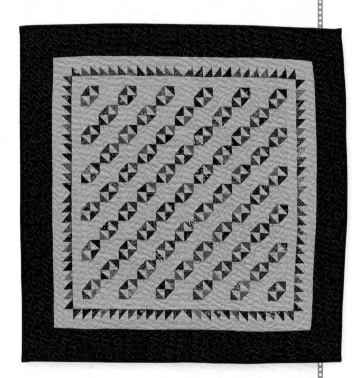

Making the Blocks

Follow the steps in "Making the Blocks" on page 87 using the tan and assorted 2" squares. Trim the 340 units to 1¼" square. Arrange and sew four half-square-triangle units together to make 61 blocks that measure 2" square, including seam allowances.

Constructing the Quilt

Finish as for the larger quilt, beginning with "Constructing the Pieced Border" on page 88. The completed quilt top should measure 26½" square.

QUILTMAKING BASICS

Quiltmaking is the result of fabrics, tools, and skills coming together in a wonderful combination. With the right fabrics, the proper tools, and basic sewing skills, anyone can make a quilt. The questions then become: "What are the right fabrics? What are the proper tools? And what skills are needed?" We hope to answer those questions here.

In addition, we've included specific instructions for techniques used in making the quilts in this book, such as constructing half-square-triangle units and adding mitered borders. For further assistance with any aspect of quiltmaking, we suggest that you take classes at your favorite quilt shop, check out some of the many excellent quilting books, and visit ShopMartingale.com/HowtoQuilt for free, downloadable information about topics such as rotary cutting, assembling the quilt sandwich, binding, and more.

Fabric

How to choose the right fabrics? If you're like most quilters, you probably have more than enough fabric already, and most of it could even be considered "right." But do feel free to shop! (You know you want to!) All the quilts featured in this book were designed and pieced using 1800s reproduction fabrics. Fabrics reminiscent of that time period include plaids, checks, stripes, polka dots, and shirtings, in color palettes that encompass blues, blacks, browns, madder reds and turkey reds, cheddars, bubblegum pinks, and poison greens. These are the prints and colors that we love and prefer to work with, but that shouldn't prevent you from piecing any of these quilts in fabrics that you consider to be right—perhaps batiks or even a combination of fabric styles. These will be your quilts; experiment with favorite fabrics.

Tools

The proper tools of the quiltmaking trade include rotary cutters, rulers, cutting mats, sharp scissors, all-cotton thread, and your favorite sewing machine in good working order (clean, oiled, and ready to go).

Rotary cutter and cutting mat. Always keep a sharp blade in your rotary cutter. It will help with accuracy and ensure that your fabric is cut smoothly. The cutting mat should be as large as you have space for.

Rulers. Our favorite ruler size for cutting strips and borders is the 6½" × 24" ruler, but square rulers are very handy for squaring up blocks. The 6½" and 9½" square rulers are the sizes we use most often.

Thread. We prefer 100% cotton thread to blend with the cotton fabrics in our quilts.

Skills

We all come to quiltmaking with varying skill levels and experiences, but accuracy is the most important qualification needed to successfully complete a quilt. Let's start with accuracy in cutting.

The instructions for all the projects in this book involve rotary cutting, and a standard ¼"-wide seam allowance is included in all measurements. Before you begin cutting, we suggest pressing your fabric well and putting a new blade in your rotary cutter. These are basic steps that go a long way toward successful cutting.

An accurate ¼" seam allowance is also essential in quiltmaking. Consider purchasing a ¼" presser foot for your sewing machine. Whether you use a ¼" foot or a standard foot, take the time to test your accuracy before you begin piecing your project. To check accuracy, follow these steps.

1 Cut three 1½" × 4" strips.

2 Sew the strips together. Press the seam allowances toward the outer strips.

3 Using a ruler, measure the width of the center strip. It should measure 1". If your center strip is larger than 1", your seam allowance is too narrow. If your center strip is smaller than 1", your seam allowance is too wide. Cut new strips and repeat until the center strip measures exactly 1".

You can also use ¼" graph paper to check your seam allowance. Place a piece of the graph paper under the presser foot and sew on the first ¼" line. Affix a piece of painter's tape or ¼" quilter's tape along the edge of the paper. Remove the graph paper and sew three strips together using the seam guide and check the center strip for accuracy. Once you know it's in the correct position, build up the seam guide with another layer or two of tape.

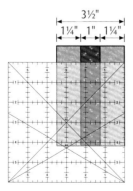

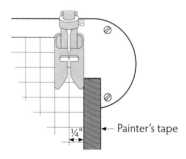
← Painter's tape

After sewing seams accurately, pressing becomes the next important step. Recommended pressing directions for seam allowances are included throughout the project instructions. Remember, you are pressing to set seams, not ironing the wrinkles out of a shirt.

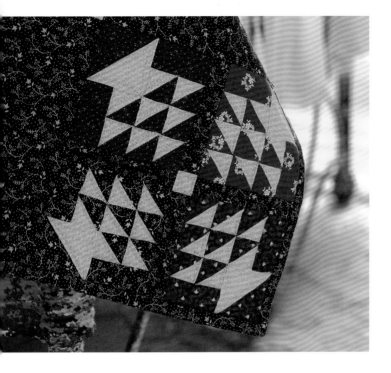

In the steps that follow, we've used 1" finished half-square-triangle units as an example.

1 Cut a light and a dark square, 1¼" larger than the desired finished size. In this case, cut the squares 2¼" × 2¼".

2 With a pencil or fabric marker and ruler, draw a diagonal line from corner to corner on the wrong side of the lighter 2¼" square.

3 Place the marked square on the dark 2¼" square with right sides together. Align the raw edges and sew ¼" from both sides of the marked line.

Mark diagonal.
Sew ¼" away from
each side of the line.

4 Cut on the marked line. You'll have two identical half-square-triangle units. Press seam allowances toward the darker triangle.

Cut on
marked line.

Press.

Half-Square-Triangle Units

We love half-square-triangle units, as you can see from our quilts! They add so much to a simple block. There are many different methods and tools available for making them, and you may already have a favorite technique. If so, feel free to use it. For these projects, we've generally used the technique of piecing the units from layered squares, without cutting triangles first.

We've also provided cutting options for some projects in which purchased triangle papers would be a good option. We like the Star Singles papers, designed by Liz Eagen of Spinning Star Design, for ease and accuracy and often use them in our quiltmaking. They make several identical half-square-triangle units at a time. When piecing Kentucky Baskets (page 64), we recommend Primitive Gatherings ¾" half-square-triangle paper, designed by Lisa Bongean. Both are widely available at quilt shops and online.

When making half-square-triangle units without the papers, we cut squares oversized and trim the final units after pressing. This guarantees complete accuracy.

5 Using a square ruler, trim the units to 1½" square, aligning the 45° line of your ruler with the seam. Make sure that the unit under the ruler extends beyond the 1½" marks and trim the right and top edges with your rotary cutter. Rotate the unit 180°, align the newly cut edges with the 1½" marks, and trim the right and top edges.

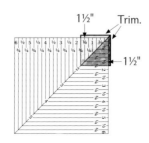 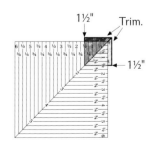

Mitered Borders

Once the blocks have been pieced together, it's time to add the borders to your quilt. There are many lovely border prints and stripes available, often with large floral motifs, that just call out for mitering. Mitered borders require extra length, and we use a formula to determine the length of fabric needed. First measure the width and length of your quilt through the middle. Decide how wide you want the border to be, and then fill in the blanks.

$$\underline{\hspace{3cm}} + (2 \times \underline{\hspace{3cm}}) + 5"$$

Length (or width)   Width of the border
of the quilt

Note that sometimes you may want to match a design at the corners. In these cases, cut the borders even longer to allow for matching the motifs before cutting the borders to the final length.

Follow these steps to ensure a well-mitered border.

1. Center and pin a border strip to one side of the quilt top. Sew the border strip to the quilt top using a ¼" seam allowance, starting and stopping ¼" from the edge. Backstitch at the beginning and end to secure the stitches. Press the seam allowances toward the border strip.

2. Repeat step 1 for each side of the quilt.

3. Fold the quilt diagonally with right sides together; align the raw edges of two adjacent border strips. Pin the two borders together.

4. Place a long acrylic ruler along the folded edge of the quilt. Align the 45° line of the ruler with the border stitching line. With a pencil, draw a line from the point where the ¼" seamline begins to the raw edge of the border strip. Pin along this line to hold the two borders in place. Lift one border strip and check to see if the miter is correct.

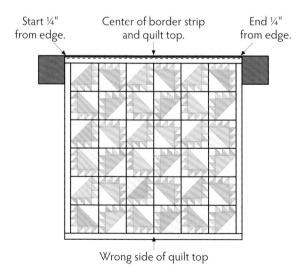

Start ¼"   Center of border strip   End ¼"
from edge.   and quilt top.   from edge.

Wrong side of quilt top

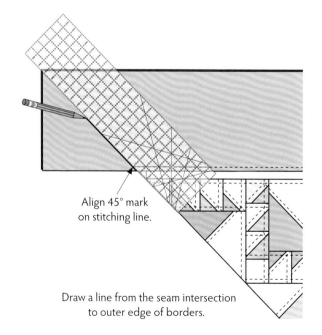

Align 45° mark
on stitching line.

Draw a line from the seam intersection
to outer edge of borders.

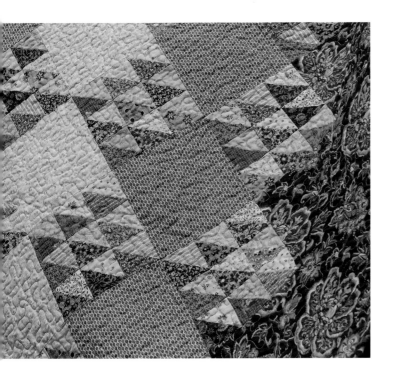

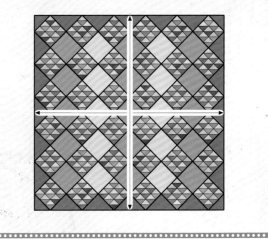

MEASURING FOR BORDERS

Always measure your quilt before cutting borders. The cutting instructions for each of our projects indicates the lengths to cut, but this is based on a consistently accurate ¼" seam allowance and perfect piecing throughout the quilt top.

Measure the quilt from top to bottom through the center to find the length, and measure from side to side through the center to find the width.

5 Beginning at the end of the border seam, sew along the pencil line to the edge of the borders. Open the borders to see if the seam lies flat and any design motifs line up. If the corner is sewn correctly, fold back on the diagonal again and trim, leaving a ¼" seam allowance. Press the seam allowances open.

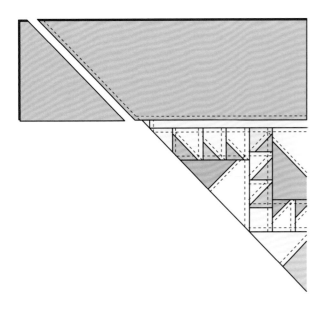

6 Repeat steps 3–5 for the remaining four corners.

Quilting

Your top is complete, so now it's time to prepare it for quilting. For many of us, that means making a backing and passing the project on to a machine quilter. The pattern instructions provide our yardage recommendations for a pieced backing. They allow for at least 3" to 4" extra on each side of the quilt, or a backing that's 6" to 8" larger than the finished quilt dimensions.

Binding

We most often use a double-fold, straight-grain binding on our quilts, but we cut our strips 1⅞" wide, which is slightly narrower than what is often suggested. We find this width provides a nice tight binding and apparently is historically accurate for our reproduction quilts. Each project includes the number of binding strips to cut, and the yardage is enough to cut 2½"-wide strips if you prefer, either across the fabric width or on the bias.

We have learned that binding cut on the lengthwise grain is not recommended. Crossgrain strips have more flexibility and stretch, ensuring that your quilt will lie flat when bound. Sew the strips end to end to make the continuous binding you will need.

DON'T FORGET A LABEL

Now that your quilt is finished, please remember to add a label. Some things to include, in addition to your full name, are the date you began the quilt, the date you completed it, your hometown, the name of the quilter (if not you), and the name of the recipient (if the quilt is a gift).

ACKNOWLEDGMENTS

First and foremost, thank you to Jennifer Keltner and Karen Burns of Martingale for believing in us not just once, but twice! Thank you also to the staff at Martingale for your help and assistance throughout this process.

It takes many hands to bring our quilts to completion. Paula designs the quilt, and Mary Ellen pieces most of the tops, but once the top is done the quilt is out of our hands. We are very fortunate to have the help of many very talented quilters who are willing to work with us and meet our deadlines. A special thank you to Marcella Pickett and Margie Love of Crooked Creek Quilts, Cathy Peters with Palm Tree Quilting, Sharon Dixon of Katy T-Shirt Quilts, and Pat Meeks for making our quilts look so beautiful with your outstanding quilting. An additional thank you to Pat Meeks, who stepped in at the last minute and pieced, quilted, and bound the Pioneer Life quilt.

Finally, thank you to our loyal fans and followers—our fellow quilters—who have supported us on this journey.

ABOUT THE AUTHORS

Paula Barnes (right) and Mary Ellen Robison (left) met more than 20 years ago when they both moved to the same street in Katy, Texas. Paula taught quilting classes at the local quilt shop, and Mary Ellen was the devoted student. They quickly formed a friendship that went beyond their love of quilting and reproduction fabric to become Red Crinoline Quilts.

Although they met in Texas, each one comes from a different part of the country. Mary Ellen was born and raised in New York, while Paula is from Georgia. Theirs is a true North-South friendship.

Mary Ellen and her husband, Peter, live in St. Petersburg, Florida, where she divides her time between sewing quilts for Red Crinoline Quilts, cruising, and traveling to see her three children and their families— Megan, son-in-law Brian, and new grandson Adam in Louisville, Kentucky; Brett, daughter-in-law Meredith, and granddaughters Sydney and Julianne in Ballston Lake, New York; and Caitlin in Tampa, Florida. Paula lives in the Houston area and is mom to three grown daughters, Alison, Ashley, and Amy; mother-in-law to three sons-in-law, David, Robert, and Alex; and grandmother (or MiMi) to granddaughter Sophie and grandson John.

Paula began teaching quilting in 1989 in Dallas, and now travels throughout the US, teaching and lecturing at quilt guilds and local quilt shops. You can contact her at Red Crinoline Quilts (info@redcrinolinequilts.com).